Heseltine as politician has always been hard to ignore. He does look the part. US Senators are portrayed on the cinema either by Robert Redford (Joe Biden of Delaware) or by Charles Laughton (Chuck Mathias of Rhode Island) – good-looking idealists or dilapidated cynics. Congressmen and MPs are, more often than not, portrayed on film and television as middle-aged men on the make who betray their wives and neglect their constituents. In this country, politicians have enjoyed a bad press. Cecil Parkinson is better known for his love life than for the part he played in Mrs Thatcher's election victory in 1983, Jack Profumo put his stamp on the Macmillan years, while John Stonehouse might have sprung from the pen of Jeffrey Archer. Michael Heseltine has been happily free of scandal. His hair, his suits and his conference oratory have cast him in the role of Action Man.

About the Author

Julian Critchley is the Conservative MP for Aldershot. He has written a number of bestsellers including COLLECTIVE SECURITY, WARNING'S RESPONSE, THE NORTH ATLANTIC ALLIANCE AND THE SOVIET UNION IN THE 1980s and most recently, WESTMINSTER BLUES.

Heseltine

The Unauthorised Biography

Julian Critchley

CORONET BOOKS
Hodder and Stoughton

British Library C.I.P.

Critchley, Julian, *1930–*
  Heseltine: the unauthorised biography.
  1. Great Britain. Politics.
  Heseltine, Michael – Biographies
  I. Title
  941.085'092'4

  ISBN 0-340-43081-8

Printed and bound in Great Britain for Hodder and Stoughton Paperbacks, a division of Hodder and Stoughton Limited, Mill Road, Dunton Green, Sevenoaks, Kent TN13 2YA (Editorial Office: 47 Bedford Square, London WC1B 3DP) by Cox and Wyman Limited, Reading, Berks.

Contents

Acknowledgements

I should like to thank John Eppstein, OBE, and Shaun Tyndale-Biscoe for their researches on my behalf, and my secretary Mrs Angela Bayfield for typing the manuscript.

Also, together with the publisher, I am grateful to the following for permission to quote: Basil Blackwell (*The Thatcher Government* by Peter Riddell); Philip Norman; the *Observer*; *The Times* (articles by Geoffrey Smith and John Young).

'*The best mirror is an old friend.*' Anon.

Prologue

I bumped into Michael Heseltine on the staircase in Pembroke College, Oxford, early in October 1951. I recognised him immediately. Our paths had already crossed twice – in 1943 when my prep school, Brockhurst, had been obliged to share a large house in Staffordshire called Broughton Hall with a prep school of that name. Michael was a Broughton boy with whom I had few dealings save to sell him a model warship at what he later described to my Aldershot constituents as 'an exorbitant price'. If so, it was an unusual victory on my part.

The rival schools coexisted uncomfortably, the two headmasters came to blows, and the litigation drove the desert war from the front pages of the tabloids. Heseltine, aged eleven, made his first public appearance in the witness box, called on behalf of his headmaster, Kenneth Thompson. After twelve months John Park took his boys five miles across country to Maer Hall, and what small contact I had with Michael was broken.

We both went on to Shrewsbury School, but to different houses. I was two years older and the rigid customs of the school discouraged friendships with younger boys, especially if they were not in the same house. I can remember one conversation behind the goal posts. He was tall, lanky, a touch uncoordinated, with close-cropped fair hair. Three years later in Oxford he looked little different. We greeted each other as long-lost friends, a reunion which we celebrated

1

with a glass of sweet sherry in my room. It was to be the start of a strong friendship.

I was thus better placed than anyone else to observe his Oxford career. Until he reached the heights of the Union Society, I could match his progress, about which there soon appeared to be an inevitability. Heseltine flowered at Oxford in a way which could only have come as a surprise to his schoolmasters. At Broughton he did not seem to amount to much; at Shrewsbury he was positively undistinguished. He was not a scholar; he could not kick a ball; he was not made a house monitor. His reputation in his house, Moser's Hall, such as it was, never spilt over into the school itself, and his bearing did not appeal to the more conventional school-master. To be fair, it should be said that Shrewsbury School in the late 'forties was as hidebound as it was inhospitable, conditions which served as a nursery for iconoclasts of the like of Richard Ingrams. It was a school for trams and not for buses.

One of the school's traditions is the writing of regular 'confidential reports' by each study monitor on the junior members of his study. Heseltine's reports while at Moser's have come to light.

At the end of his first summer term someone wrote 'useless', but then attempted to erase the comment. In his second summer term his study monitor wrote '. . . has a certain spirit but incorrigibly idle and very reluctant to do anything when told'.

In his first term, however, one B.L.H. Wilson wrote of Heseltine, 'he is rebellious, objectionable, idle, imbecilic, inefficient, antagonising, untidy, lunatic, albino, conceited, inflated, impertinent, underhand, lazy and smug. But cheerful and probably rudimentally good-natured'. No man is a hero to his study monitor.

At the end of his third summer term at Wolfenden's Shrewsbury his then-study monitor wrote, '. . . very much the budding businessman'. Apparently Heseltine used to buy old pop bottles from boys at half the deposit price, go downtown and collect. The following term someone wrote, 'Michael Heseltine has his own ideas about most things and if he wants anything he will get it, no matter how he does it.' In his last year Heseltine captained the 2nd House cricket and football teams (he was no athlete), and joined the Economics Upper Sixth Form. As a study monitor himself, he wrote on his last night at school, 'I will come back to the place that means so much, and to which I can repay so little.' That was one promise he has kept.

Both of us chose Pembroke for its ease of entry. In those days it was the sole college not to require the passing of an entrance exam. Matriculation, derived from the results of the Higher School Certificate when taken with a dialect-free accent and the wearing, in my case at least, of my father's suit, was deemed to be an adequate qualification. Some stress was placed upon the interview, which would have provided few difficulties for either of us. A more egalitarian age would have demanded 'straight As', a qualification which might well have excluded the young Michael Heseltine or Julian Critchley.

Pembroke was an obscure college, anchored in the lee of Christ Church, famous for the brief residence of Dr Johnson. The master was Homes Dudden, then in his seventies and bedridden. Responsibility for the college fell to the senior tutor, R.B. McCallum, a Lowland Scot of the Liberal persuasion, who was responsible in 1947 for the first of the general election books. As both Michael and I had decided to read PPE – philosophy, politics and economics – we were taught politics by McCallum. Economics was the province of Neville Ward-Perkins, sadly to die comparatively young, while philosophy, to which we paid scant attention, was taught by a Mr McNab. Pembroke was a pretty place, placid and undemanding, whose undergraduates were on the worthy side with a taste for wearing college ties and sporting scarves. Michael Heseltine was to prove an exotic creature for so provincial a park.

I suppose that at the start I held the advantage. Two years

older, I had spent the three years since quitting Shrewsbury kicking my heels in Hampstead and amusing myself with the local Young Conservatives, who were taking advantage of the ladders of political opportunity let down by Lord Woolton into the tennis-playing suburbs, and living in Paris, ostensibly studying *la civilisation française* at the Sorbonne. I drank cheap wine, subscribed to *France Soir* and sported a silk dressing-gown. Over my mantel, on which were soon to be displayed my invitations, I hung a reproduction of Renoir's 'Girl on a Swing'.

Michael, on the other hand, had come up to Oxford straight from school after a summer spent in and about Swansea. His room had a Salopian severity about it, relieved only by invitations as numerous as my own.

From the moment of our meeting we plotted our course. 'Pemmy' was plainly too small a stage for his talents. The university was to be the marketplace for his ambition. Oxford was to be the antechamber of his career in politics, a career which had as its goal No. 10 Downing Street. A good degree was relatively unimportant; Michael even then knew that he would 'go into business', which would permit him to make the necessary fortune. What was important was to be elected president of the Union, that traditional stepping-stone to political success. The presidency was unattainable save through politics. It was plainly necessary to join a political party whose vote would be deliverable throughout the progress of election to committees, to office and then to the presidency itself. Which one should we join?

Entirely predictably, we joined the Oxford Tories, or OUCA – Oxford University Conservative Association, to give its full title – a consequence not of any intellectual effort or conscious choice, but one of upbringing. Michael came from a middle-middle-class Swansea family who lived in a detached house 'up the Gower Road', the smart end of that otherwise undistinguished seaport. Michael's father was a wartime half-colonel who had become general manager of Dawnay's, a local steelworks; his mother was the daughter of a Swansea man who had made, and largely lost, a good deal of money exporting coal. The Heseltines were 'respectable Welsh', a description which in Swansea and the rest of Wales still has a ring to it. Michael's education had been conventional and expensive. He was a middle-class boy brought up as a Conservative; so, too, was I. We could not have joined any other party.

Michael made no secret of his ambition. I had never met anyone as determined as he was to make his mark. We used to dine frequently together at a restaurant down by the station called 'Long John's', the owner of which had served in the army with Michael's father during the war. Mr Silver would knock 50% off the bill to encourage Michael's attendance in the hope, perhaps, of attracting university custom. I can remember Michael charting his course on the back of an envelope: he divided the last half of the century into decades, against which he marked the position he would have reached. Against the 'nineties he wrote 'Downing Street'. Ian Josephs, a mutual friend, who had also come up to Pembroke in October 1951, tells the story of his sitting next to Michael in hall on the first night of term. They did not speak, but Josephs' attention was drawn by Heseltine striking his spoon three times against his glass. 'I am practising', he explained, 'to become the president of the Union'. Josephs, who had never heard of the Union, was impressed.

The young Heseltine was a very green apple. His failure to shine at school, where he had found the water too cold and the company uncongenial, had triggered his ambition. And success at Oxford could be won by means unsuited to the flannelled enthusiasms of Wolfenden's Shrewsbury where the individual was subordinated to the House, and athletic prowess was accorded undue prestige. A university political career, rising first to the top of the Oxford Tory party, then climbing the ladder of Union office, would enable him to attract national attention, and, armed with an *Isis* Idol – a profile carried by that magazine, which was the ultimate accolade of the university's public life – he could make his way in the world beyond Oxford. I wanted much the same, but in the end became a spectator of Michael's progress.

Later on in his Oxford career Michael acquired, as a gift from his enemies, the nickname 'Michael Philistine', a jibe that struck home. He came from a comfortable home but one where books were in no way conspicuous. Four years at Shrewsbury may have done something for his physique (Salopians were so fit on discharge that the benefits lasted for many of us into early middle age) and for his general knowledge, but at Pembroke he appeared gauche and culturally ill-equipped. He was never bookish, which may have been a consequence of his mild dyslexia, a condition which was not to be diagnosed until some twenty years later. We were passionate cinemagoers, although whereas I plumped for French films which were the 'fifties equivalent of watching Channel 4, Michael preferred Westerns. We sat through *High Noon* at least half-a-dozen times. Gary Cooper's deserted sheriff facing four hired killers, who had arrived on the midday train, only to emerge triumphant and vindicated, had its peculiar allegorical appeal. Michael had no music, although he did have a tendency to weep in Swansea cinemas whenever the Welsh anthem, 'We'll Keep a Welcome', was sung, which was often. Painting, sculpture, the decorative arts were *terra incognita*.

He was also impatient with authority of all kinds. Michael was no conformist despite his adherence to the Conservative Party. Had his parents been poorer, he would have been a grammar school recruit into Clement Attlee's Labour Party. Even in 1951 both Michael and I identified not with the gentlemen of the Tory Party but with its players. The gents were the unreconstructed Tories, social snobs who had not put their name to the postwar consensus which had been arrived at between Churchill and Attlee in the last year of the coalition government. The players were the 'progressive Tories' such as David Eccles or Iain Macleod, who understood the need to keep the Tory Party up to date and, in particular, the desirability of full employment. It is ironic that today the tables have been turned, conflict within the party being between the traditionalists, among whose ranks Michael is to be found, and the 'Thatcherites', fundamentalists with the urge to make people pull up their socks. But in the early 'fifties we looked to Robert Boothby, not to Waldron Smithers, and Michael was to import the dispute between the party's left and right into the hitherto placid waters of OUCA, the president of which had been, not two years previously, Miss Margaret Roberts (Somerville).

At this distance it is not too hard to list the qualities and defects of the young Heseltine. They have not changed. Superficially, it did not take him long to acquire the gloss, the patina which the nation has come to know and love. He grew his hair and found a tailor. His most obvious characteristic both then and now was his determination which was complemented by his stamina. His friends may have played at politics, but not Michael. He had the ability to set targets and to achieve them; more importantly, perhaps, he could identify his relative weaknesses and set about rectifying them. It was not necessary to demonstrate a knowledge of political philosophy, or even dialectical skill, but it was vital to be able to make a good speech. And Michael was no orator. He was quick-witted but his formal oratory, if his early performances at the Union were a guide, was wooden. It was at this juncture that Mrs Stella Gatehouse came to the rescue. A chain-smoking parson's wife of indeterminate age and cheerful disposition, she had been hired by the Oxford City Conservative Association to run weekly speakers' classes for Tory undergraduates. I do not know who was responsible for so far-sighted a decision – perhaps the party's area agent based in Wessex? – but it was a handsome gift from Town to Gown, and one which, in Heseltine's case, was to pay a handsome dividend.

Heseltine's skills as a speaker were polished by Mrs Gatehouse and practised upon the unsuspecting. On Wednesday afternoons ambitious young Conservatives would assemble in a dingy upstairs room above a milk bar to be taught how to take the pebble out of their mouths. Stella Gatehouse, a cigarette hanging from her lips, would call upon her flock to perform. Five minutes without notes on 'Setting the People Free' or the 'Cost of Socialism', topics culled from the Conservative Central Office notes on current politics. We were told to stand erect, synchronise our few gestures and project our voices to the back of the hall. Those in whom she had some confidence were sent out to address afternoon meetings of the local Tory ladies. Michael and I would drive to the village hall in a remote Oxfordshire village and face twenty-five or so middle-aged women of the kind who made up the foot soldiers of the Mothers' Union, with the parson's wife in the chair. As the topic chosen did not seem to matter much, we would rehearse our next Union speech: ten minutes on 'A Woman's Place . . .' or 'The University of Life is to be preferred to the University of Oxford'. No one seemed to mind. Some knitted, others slept. What we did learn was to sit down the moment we heard the sound of rattling tea cups. To this day no Tory speaker will fight against the chink of crockery.

Mrs Gatehouse's favourites were invited to her Banbury vicarage for tea on Sunday. These were jolly occasions on sunlit lawns accompanied by large slices of farmhouse cake and the ubiquitous victoria sponge. Once a year or so one of our number would be invited to preach in her husband's church. This remarkable honour fell to Michael, who was adjured in the name of the Almighty to avoid politics. A handful of his friends, who had certainly not been inside a church since the compulsory services of their schooldays, attended evensong in the village church. A dozen farm labourers' wives, a few half-colonels and their ladies, and four undergraduates, were treated to a tirade in which mention was made of Churchill, Roosevelt, Stalin and 'a bonfire of controls'. The Reverend Gatehouse did not seem to mind after all.

Michael Heseltine could soon make an effective five minute political speech, an ability which has never let him down since. His striking appearance and Aryan good looks ('Von Heseltine' to his enemies) were not easily overlooked at OUCA meetings, where it was not long before the founder and chairman of the renegade Blue Ribbon Club had become chairman of OUCA, elected by the membership and not by the committee. Cabinet ministers began to appear more frequently on the OUCA card. On one occasion, as secretary of OUCA, I had arranged for a visit by Mr Henry Brooke. He was due, or so we believed, to speak on a Wednesday evening. On the Tuesday Michael and I were in the bar of the Randolph Hotel having attended an open meeting of the Labour Club, where Michael had spent five minutes condemning socialism. We spotted Henry Brooke in the restaurant, gloomily toying with a chop. He had come up at our bidding, found an empty hall and was recruiting himself prior to taking the last train home. I had made a mistake in the date. Michael and I crept out of the hotel, leaving the great man to his ruminations.

The Oxford Union is the temple to precocity. Housed in a hideously redbrick, late-Victorian complex behind the Cornmarket, it is the best-known student debating society in the world – the 'nursery' of prime ministers. The bust of Harold Macmillan gazes with his quizzical good humour at the antics of generations of clever young men, licensed to perform, strangers – if only on Thursday evenings during term – to modesty. The presidency is determined by vote at the end of each of the year's three terms, together with the less important offices of treasurer and librarian. There are also two committees, library and standing, on to which the aspirants strive to be elected. The Union, which is a self-regulating society with dons among its trustees, combines the function of club, library and debating society. It is administered by a steward and staff, and has a history of financial crises regularly overcome. In his climb to the top, Michael Heseltine began as an orator and ended as an entrepreneur. Elected to the presidency at the end of his last Trinity term, in 1954, he persuaded the ever-compliant Pembroke authorities to permit him to stay up for an extra term. This was an unusual favour for an undergraduate – and Pembroke have retained their soft spot for their charismatic alumnus, making him a fellow of the college in December 1986.

Michael stepped easily from library to standing committee and then to office. His opportunity came when he was treasurer. The Union's finances were even direr than had been expected, but Michael had, or so it was believed, the answer. He persuaded the steward, Leslie Crawte, to open up the cellars beneath the debating hall. After much toing and froing, permission was won from his fellow officers, and coats of white paint were applied to the warren of bricklined cellars. Michael and his friend Sarah Rothschild had, in the meantime, been taken up by the Dockers, Bernard and Norah, who at that time were national celebrities. Michael and Sarah had also been featured in the gossip columns of national papers. How they met I cannot remember, but Michael proposed that Norah Docker should be invited to open the cellars.

This idea was greeted by some tut-tutting on the part of Bryan Magee and Tyrell Burgess, but they were obliged to give way to the clamour of the more vulgar. The Dockers turned up in Oxford in their gold-plated Daimler (escorted by half the national press), and Michael asked Norah for the first dance. They must have been separated by forty years, but at the end of the dance Lady Docker went up to Sir Bernard, who was a kind old fruit unused to dancing, and said 'Oh Bernard, dear, this nice young man here tells me they're twelve hundred pounds short on paying for these cellars. Couldn't you sign a cheque for him? He's so nice!' Looking very aggrieved, Bernard Docker did exactly that.

After such a triumph, the Union was clearly ready for a period of military government. Sir Peter Tapsell, MP, at that time a Labour Party supporter, claims to be the author of Michael's presidential speech, on the success of which everything hung. Many hands cooperated in the drafting, for he

10

was, and not for the last time, the man on a white horse. Doubts as to his intellectual abilities, or even as to his talent to amuse the Union, were stilled, and a kind of consensus was reached whereby it was agreed that the Union might well be saved by the election of so charismatic a figure. In the event, Michael was easily elected against a not very impressive opponent.

The Trinity term of 1954, culminating as it did in his Union success, was for Michael a time of unrelieved good fortune. We had moved at the beginning of the Oxford year into digs in St John's Street, the most fashionable part of town. Pembroke was unvisited. Not even the imminence of the schools (finals) could cast a shadow. Michael had done enough work in history and economics to get by; what was more difficult was political and moral philosophy. Once again his friends came to the rescue with the loan of essays and the gift of impromptu tutorials. For perhaps a fortnight he swotted, abandoning the Union and Playhouse bars, the Oxford cinemas and the weekend visits to dine at Weston Manor, a smart country club. He got a second. I went down at the end of the summer, but Michael invited me back to speak at the Union that autumn in a debate on Ireland. He presided over the debate with aplomb, and, clearly, his regime had been a success. The cellars still made money, membership was up, and the gossip columns wrote frequently of the doings of Sarah and Michael. Anthony Howard wrote his *Isis* Idol and Beverley Baxter in the *Evening Standard* wrote of him as a future prime minister. Michael finally quit the university at the end of the Michaelmas term, in receipt of his glittering prizes; the lean years were immediately ahead of him.

The Oxford of thirty years ago has been lent enchantment by the passage of time. By October 1951 the great men and women of the immediate postwar generation had departed. Their aroma lingered on. The first five years of peace had absorbed the battle-hardened, many of whom had brought both scars and wives to Oxford. The ex-officers had, generally, worked hard and were not prepared to play the undergrad. Brideshead was not revisited until the late forties. Michael Heseltine's Oxford reverberated to the sound of Ken Tynan who had, in the time-honoured manner, set out to shock the respectable and had succeeded beyond even his expectations. Tynan had written, acted, and performed at the Union. He had come to Oxford the illegitimate son of a Birmingham businessman; he left it as a national celebrity. Heseltine could not write, and certainly could not act, but he was determined to become president of the Union.

Robin Day had taken the Union by storm. Jeremy Thorpe who, twenty years later, was to come such a cropper, had played the showman there to great effect. His panache, his oratory and his Liberal vote had carried him to the presidency despite an investigation for corrupt election practices, of which he was acquitted. The diary columns of the middleweight press were devoted to him. Peter Kirk, later to be knighted by Ted Heath for his political services in respect of our entry into Europe, had been a prominent Conservative. Anthony Wedgwood Benn, Peter Parker and Michael Elliot were among the more glittering, while Shirley Catlin, later to become Williams, was, in the opinion of the Union barflies, more than likely to become Britain's first woman prime minister. Margaret Roberts had not braved the debating society, and was unremembered. But this was the roll call of the departed: anyone with ambition in October '51 did not want for rivals.

Oxford in the 'fifties enjoyed a much higher proportion of public-school boys to grammar than is the case today. Probably a third of the university had been to fee-paying schools, Old Etonians went to Christ Church ('the House'), where many of them joined OUCA, thus making up the largest contribution in terms of votes in the OUCA elections. Wykehamists went to New College, Harrovians to Queen's and Rugbeians to University. Balliol discriminated only in favour of brains, and Pembroke in favour of Old Salopians.

Grammar school boys were spread evenly throughout the university.

An article in *Isis* at that time divided the undergraduates (the word 'student' was unthinkable) into four categories: hearty, tarty, arty and smarty. The hearties, of whom Pembroke had its share, ran and rowed. So vigorous an addiction, redolent of compulsory runs through filthy Shropshire farmyards, did not appeal to Michael or to me. The smarties in their brown trousers and sporting floppy fair hair came either from the House or Magdalen. They took refuge in dining clubs like the Bullingdon and Carlton, from the windows of which they could despise their fellows. The hearties took no interest whatever in politics. The smarties did – on occasion coming to the aid of their class in OUCA, but only rarely at the Union.

The arties who were the actors, poets and scribblers of all kinds were a leftish minority that tended to join the Union, when they were not rehearsing for an OUDS production of *Hamlet* or pursuing the young Maggie Smith who was a regular at the Playhouse. They had, as it were, a foot in both camps. The tarties, which is admittedly a less happy description, was a catch-all term for those of us who sought fame, or notoriety, on the university stage with the help of love affairs which were almost invariably heterosexual, or the great Union speech on a Thursday evening, a speech which would take Oxford by the throat.

I suppose we were numbered among the arty/tarties. Ian Josephs, who shared a room in college with Michael for two years and afterwards went into business with him, claims that the three of us were asked, probably over the soused herrings at Long John's, what we wanted out of life. Josephs said 'pleasure', I plumped for 'fame', and Michael for 'power'. I leave the likes of Anthony Clare to make what they want of that.

The first two years of life at Oxford made only one demand: 'prelims', preliminary examinations which were held at the end of the first year. Michael failed his first time, but passed at the end of the first term of his second year. Prelims were a low hurdle, and there was nothing between them and finals which, at the end of the third year, lay so far ahead as to be virtually invisible. In search of fame and power, we quickly attained pleasure.

If we deferred to the three tutorials a week, it was more from courtesy than from love of learning. Enough work was done, usually by copying out chunks of Samuelson for Mr Ward-Perkins' benefit, to keep the dons at bay. McCallum, when asked by Michael why he had never joined the Labour Party, replied that he could never join a 'movement', which Labour was, and is, but only a party. The senior tutor had no good opinion of Dick Crossman, a frequent guest at the major Union debates, who, sporting black suede shoes with his dinner jacket, was the performer we most admired. 'A dreadful man,' was McCallum's opinion; 'he has debauched his undergraduates.' I can now see what he meant. Lectures, save for those given by Alan Bullock, Lord Pakenham, and A.J.P. Taylor, were ignored; they certainly were of no use for picking up girls, earnest scholars who gave us nothing save a glimpse of a blue stocking.

The pattern of our days was swiftly set: a long drawn out breakfast with the heavier newspapers, coffee somewhere in town, a sandwich lunch at the Union, and the choice of Oxford's four cinemas, only one of which would be showing *High Noon*. The evenings were for parties. Heseltine and Josephs would invite a selection of celebrities to their room in college: politicos like Anthony Howard, Norman St John Stevas, who had come to Oxford from Cambridge while on the road to Rome, Bryan Magee and Paddy Mayhew, a patrician Tory who had been elected president of the Union and who was to reenter Michael's life thirty or more years later in his role as the Solicitor General who wrote the leaked letter. Josephs provided the more Bohemian undergraduates and, just as important, the girls.

Oxford before the sexual revolution of the 'sixties contained the greater part of Philip Larkin's 'the last of the fouled-up generation'. We thought about sex much of the time but did very little about it. This was as much due to the shortage of girls in the city – undergraduettes were few in number and serious-minded – as it was to the fact of our middle-class upbringing. We imported our home town girl-friends who were put up at hotels and entertained at great expense, or trawled the town for nurses from the Radcliffe and the General Hospital. I owned a Model-T Ford, purch-ased from a Hertfordshire chicken farmer for one hundred pounds, which Michael and I used for flying visits to friends in London and for drives to Abingdon to the Rose and Crown, where we would spend the evening admiring the landlady's very pretty daughter in competition with Bruce Montgomery, who later achieved fame as Edmund Crispin. Ian Josephs suffered from fewer 'hang-ups' than we did. Perhaps he did not share our fear of rejection. Whatever the reason, he had a way with the girls, many of whom he introduced to us both. Although we boasted of our con-quests, we were slow to go into detail. All too often, necking and not intercourse provided the climax, an act of passion that took place on the back seat among a cloud of chicken feathers.

Michael often borrowed my car. A succession of Dianas and Bridgets was interrupted by a Portuguese countess but she returned to Lisbon and failed to respond to his letters. A beautiful Swede and an old flame of mine were his partners at commem. balls and college dances. Sarah Rothschild, his great chum when he became president of the Union, was the belle of the university. On one occasion he was let down by a London girl who refused to board the 'fornication flyer', the name given to the 6.10 from Paddington. Unabashed, Hesel-tine advertised for a partner in *Isis*, and took his pick of the applicants. His striking looks did not always guarantee success; one of the less impressed told me that she much preferred people to look at her, not at him.

A life of pleasure was not permitted to pass without an eye being kept on the main chance. Heseltine maintained what today would be called 'a high profile', seeing and being seen about the university, speaking from the floor at the Union in the hope of a presidential invitation to speak 'on the paper'. More particularly, he would attend the frequent meetings of OUCA, meetings which were addressed by itinerant ministers and by the more popular Tory MPs.

I would spend part of each summer as Michael's guest in Swansea. Michael's father was a military-looking man, moustached and well-regarded. We were once driven by him to some business meeting in Cardiff. Michael and I had lunch together in an hotel, and, tired of waiting, dozed during the early afternoon in the lounge. No doubt we had been up much of the previous night, arguing the toss. Colonel Heseltine seemed gravely shocked at what he saw as his son's lassitude. The siesta was not a local custom. However, it should be said that lethargy is not one of Michael's failings.

Michael's mother had been born in Swansea. She would entertain her friends to afternoon tea, functions which Michael and I were sometimes pleased to attend. Once I interrupted the conversation to ask if anyone knew Dylan Thomas. Silence fell. Mrs Heseltine, pouring herself another cup of tea, said firmly, 'We don't talk about Dylan Thomas in Swansea.' The poet was not celebrated up the Gower Road. But we talked about everything else, and the Heseltines were kind and hospitable. The Heseltine house, which was large, 'thirties suburban with a comfortable garden, gave access to the Gower peninsula, one of the first parts of Britain to be designated an area of outstanding natural beauty. We would join a party of Michael's friends and spend our time swimming and dancing at local hops. In the intervals Michael would indulge himself in two of his hobbies: hard physical work – he was an enthusiastic knocker-down of walls and digger of ditches – and birds. An aviary had been built in the garden to accommodate a flock of exotic, multicoloured birds.

Michael, together with his younger sister, Yvonne, who

was known to the family as 'Bubbles', had been brought up comfortably in what seemed a happy home. There were few books but a good deal of self-confidence. Swansea must have provided a secure and loving foundation on which to build a career.

The Oxford Tories recruited members each term by means of their programme of speakers. The OUCA committee, which was elected on a termly basis by the membership at large, elected the officers of the association in its turn. Thus the president and secretary of OUCA were elected indirectly, a matter which was to assume an unexpected importance. The term's card for Michaelmas 1951 might well have included an open meeting, a speech by Captain Macmillan, a debate and a visit by Bob Boothby. The famous were entertained to dinner, sometimes at the Randolph itself, by the OUCA officers and their friends. The Liberals were the largest party, followed by the Conservatives; Labour divided into two, the Labour Club and the Socialist Society. Many of the politically interested joined all three parties.

Election to the committee of OUCA was plainly our first step. To this end Michael and I would turn up at every meeting and put pertinent questions to the speaker. But Michael's dialectic, and my father's Savile Row suits, were not enough to get us elected to the committee at the end of term. We were premature in our bid, and I for one was prepared to bide my time and try again next term. Not so Heseltine.

Michael seized upon the indirect method of election as a *casus belli*. It became, as the European alternative for Westland Helicopters was to do thirty years later, 'a matter of principle'. The storm in the teacup was intense. Oxford Tories, starved of controversy, immediately took sides. Whenever it appeared that interest was flagging, Michael would attack the gents from the House whose insouciance and whose politics were not to his liking. We stood again the following term for the committee, and were again defeated, this time by a narrow margin in a much bigger poll. It was at this juncture that Michael played his ace.

He proposed that the 'radicals' form their own party. The Blue Ribbon Club was conjured up by Michael, myself and a man called Oliver Crawford and, at an extraordinary public meeting held, I believe, in Exeter College, Michael was elected its president. Thus, what became known as Heseltine's Private Army took the field alongside OUCA, to which we still belonged. This unprecedented manoeuvre won Michael such renown, that he could leapfrog his rivals (and seniors) on the OUCA committee when it came to Union elections. Instead of the year which it took most ambitious undergraduates to be elected to the committee, and thus to tap the party vote for the Union elections, he needed only two terms. Actually, Heseltine had gone one better: he had risen to the top of his own party, the membership of which was barely less than that of its parent. The fact of university life whereby each year one generation is replaced by another, meant that in our second year we had only to shake the OUCA tree for the fruit to fall to the ground. I was reminded of all this by Sir Patrick Mayhew in the 'aye' lobby at the height of the Westland Affair in January 1986. 'Just like the Blue Ribbon' was Paddy's verdict.

Two years before Michael's election as president the competition had looked particularly daunting. The office had been filled by a succession of clever young men: Paddy Mayhew, a traditionally minded Tory lawyer; Sir Andrew Cunninghame, another Tory, who was to die prematurely, cutting short a promising political career; a wisecracking American called Howard Schulman, a fluent Indian, Rhagavan Iyer, and Tyrell Burgess, whose climb to the top had been the swiftest for many years. Bryan Magee, the philosopher, who was later to be elected a Labour MP and to turn to the Social Democrats, was also president. A university year behind Michael were a group of the equally talented, including Anthony Howard, who could speak as well as he could write; and Jeremy Isaacs, a saturnine Scot who was to become the Chairman of Channel 4. Gerald Kaufman was our exact contemporary.

The politicos made a club of the Union building, meeting before lunch in the bar, reading listlessly during the afternoon, usually returning to their colleagues for a meagre dinner, and then back to the Union for more beer and gossip. Michael, who was richer than most of his contemporaries thanks to the generosity of his family, would eat at one or other of the Oxford restaurants: Long John's, White's, where one could buy a dish of fried mussels and tartar sauce, the Regency or, greatly daring, risk the curries of the Taj Mahal. My Ford brought the Bear at Woodstock and the Trout at Godstowe within easy range. Whatever the venue, the conversation had a familiar ring. The chances of X, the size of the Liberal vote, the poverty of recent union debates, the dialectical skill of visitors like Ted Leather, Michael Foot and Stephen McAdden. As a subject, politics might well be followed by sex, but never by religion.

Michael did manage to straddle different worlds. Anthony Howard remembers him playing poker with Patrick Dromgoole, the theatre producer, and he was a friend of Clive Labovitch who, together with Earle White, had bought the university newspaper *Cherwell*, rival to the *Isis*. Another friend was David Hughes, the novelist, who was to marry, to the envy of his friends, the Swedish film star Mai Zetterling.

Heseltine did not always make a good first impression. Tony Howard remembers him as 'fair and Germanic-looking', a 'cold' man whose ambition was not disguised. Nevertheless, they soon became friends. Howard gives 'application' as Michael's chief characteristic, followed by 'consideration', particularly towards those people he likes. Although Tony Howard and Jeremy Isaacs were both members of the Labour Club, they decided eventually to support Michael for the presidency. What the Union needed, so they thought, was Heseltine's money-making skills, for the Union was facing yet another of its periodic financial crises.

Although canvassing for election to office and committee

was strictly forbidden, posturing was not. The rival candidates would spend more time on their speeches – from the floor, or a five-minute speech for which notice would have been given by the president, or, most important of all, a speech upon the paper – than they would on any weekly essay. Ian Josephs recalls Michael telling him that 'one day I will wow them at the party conference', and trying out a joke which was not to surface till Blackpool twenty years later about Socialists marching 'left, left, left . . .' Michael never told jokes, though in general the more talented Union politicians went in for humour; for a funny speech on a motion such as 'Rather than the Pilgrim Fathers landing on Plymouth Rock, it would have been better had Plymouth Rock landed on the Pilgrim Fathers' would add a second stage to the performer's rocket.

Shrewsbury School provided an unlikely practice ground for Heseltine's skills when, in 1952, he and I wangled an invitation to return to the school to speak at the debating society on the motion 'That this house would abolish the public schools'. Ian Josephs drove us to Shrewsbury, the three of us squeezed into his MG. Entertainment of any sort was uncommon at Shrewsbury, and the hall was packed. The chief defender of authority was Anthony Chenevix-Trench, a housemaster who was later to become headmaster of Eton. Michael opposed him – a natural alignment, considering the Heseltine discontent with authority in general, and with Shrewsbury School in particular. After a hectic debate in which home truths flew like confetti, the motion, in scenes reminiscent of the worst excesses of the French Revolution, was carried narrowly. The senior boys, by and large, sided with their masters; the juniors took revenge for their discomfort and frequent humiliation. Chenevix-Trench's taste for corporal punishment was held up by us both to ridicule.

I went down town to my hotel. Michael stayed with Mr Phillips, his one-time housemaster. Flushed with victory, I telephoned the Press Association and gave them a breathless account of what had happened.

The *Daily Mirror* rang the headmaster in the small hours and then carried the story on its front page, and the news of a public school voting to abolish itself appeared in every paper. Michael came down to breakfast in Moser's Hall quite unabashed, and proceeded to upbraid Phillips on the topic of juvenile homosexuality over the cornflakes. Mrs Phillips was driven from the room. I was accused of selling the story to the press. I had not. I was too green to know that such a thing was possible. I had made a gift of the information. The Old Salopian Society threatened expulsion, and the news of the debate even reached Australia. There was much shaking of grey Salopian heads, and it was opined that Michael Heseltine would come to no good end. He has yet to be invited to be principal guest at the school's speech day.

Michael Heseltine quit Oxford with a cheque for a thousand pounds left to him in his maternal grandfather's will – half of what remained of his one-time fortune. Ian Josephs had also come into money and they joined forces to buy a boarding house, 39 Clanricarde Gardens, a cul-de-sac on the northern side of Notting Hill Gate. In 1955 there was no security of tenure, no rent restrictions. 39 Clanricarde Gardens may one day be graced by a blue plaque, but thirty years ago it was a small step on a rickety ladder. Tall and narrow, gloomy and dilapidated, the house was divided into eighteen rooms; Heseltine lived in two of them and let the rest at two or three guineas a week.

There was also an attic room, made available, free of charge, to his friends. It was tiny and under the eaves, lit by a skylight. I lived there for a time before my marriage in October 1955. So, later, did Anthony Howard who complained of water dripping on to his bed. Not unreasonably, Michael pointed out that were Howard to pay him some rent, the leak would be stopped. The business had a turnover of fifty or sixty pounds a week.

It was for Michael a comedown after the comforts of St John's Street and the adulations of Oxford. He was threatened by National Service and, at least in part to keep the brown men at bay, he studied for his accountancy exams. But, try as he might, he was unable to cope. His financial successes were to point to his numeracy, but at the time the figures were beyond him.

Should any of his tenants fall behind with the rent, due on a Friday, Michael would fit a lock to the outside of their doors and await their return. An agreement to pay was arrived at; no one was ever put on to the street. Josephs tells of one occasion when a large American sailor, suspecting that Michael had designs upon his girlfriend (it was, in fact, the other way around), poured a pint of beer over his landlord's pyjamas. Michael beat a retreat. Life in Clanricarde Gardens was pretty sordid but it provided an income and a roof over his head. And the value of the boarding house was steadily appreciating. After a year they sold the property and bought for fourteen thousand pounds, half of which was on mortgage, the New Court Hotel in Inverness Terrace.

The Bayswater Road in the mid 'fifties had yet to feel the imprint of the Wolfenden Report on prostitution. The large Victorian terraces were shabby, and their many residential hotels doubled as 'knocking-shops' for American servicemen and others. After dark the pavements opposite the park were patrolled by an army of tarts. At the traffic lights, respectable motorists kept to the outside lane. The residents of many of the private hotels could have stepped out of *Separate Tables*; the 'guests' were, besides randy servicemen, commercial travellers and visiting provincials without much money. The New Court was indistinguishable from a hundred other such establishments.

Heseltine and Josephs brought as dowry gallons of powder-blue paint. A bevy of medical students, some of whom were friends of Michael's, were hired for as much drink as they could carry, to repaint the chocolate corridors and dingy cream public rooms of the hotel overnight. Michael, exercising his leadership qualities, greeted the dawn as paint bespattered as his men. When strongly pressed, he would, at the prompting of his friends, reluctantly open, and serve behind, the hotel's small bar. Money rarely changed hands. The New Court was not so much an hotel as a boarding house along the lines of 39 Clanricarde Gardens, but Heseltine and Josephs eventually fell out in a dispute as to whether the New Court should become a hotel or a boarding house, a difference of opinion which coincided with the reappearance of Clive Labovitch, another old Oxford friend.

Labovitch, the undergraduate who had bought *Cherwell*, is the younger son of a Leeds family which made money from the rag trade. Since he had come down he had gone into publishing, founding the Cornmarket Press and bringing out, with some success, a series of *Directories of Opportunities for Graduates* and the like. At the same time as Michael and Ian Josephs parted company and sold up, Heseltine and Labovitch joined forces. The New Court was sold to a Colonel Sinclair, an associate of Rachman's, at a handsome profit and Michael used his share to buy another boarding house in Tregunter Road and set up a property company called Bastion Constructions. In Tregunter Road Michael lived a life of luxury. His drawing-room was dominated by an enormous chandelier, his bathroom would not have disgraced the Colbys', and the flat was partly warmed by electrically charged carpets. I remember spending an uncomfortable night on the floor seeking what heat I could find. He bought a two litre Jaguar, and employed a chauffeur. The Lad had arrived. It was at this juncture that he was obliged to take the Queen's shilling.

It was typical of Michael to do everything possible to avoid national service. But since he was unable to satisfy Peat, Marwick and Mitchell as to his aptitude for accountancy, it was quite in character that he should opt for the Welsh Guards. He always did believe in nothing but the best, and chose his regiment, known in the Household Division as 'the foreign legion', for reasons of sentiment. A child of the Welsh commercial middle class, he has never spoken with a South Walian accent, although he can do a good imitation of a

Swansea docker. Michael is the kind of Welshman whom the Welsh think English, and the English are surprised to learn is Welsh. Wales casts a powerful spell over its inhabitants, and Michael is not immune. Indeed, his emotionalism is a strong element in his character and has on occasions, such as his resignation from the cabinet in January 1986 over Westland, been at war with his innate caution and taste for calculation. It is the key to understanding what makes him tick. And Michael's compassion is not just a politician's device for winning the good opinion of others; it is part of his make-up.

Michael has been silent about his national service. In the spring of 1958, after his period of initial training (which, after so many soft years, must have been hell), he unexpectedly rang the bell of my flat in Blackheath. My wife answered the door and failed to recognise him. The blond mane had fallen to some sergeant's scissors and he was as gaunt as a parade ground. His features were undistinguished; without his crowning glory, I doubt if even his mother would have known him. 'All I could see,' said my wife maliciously, 'was two pink eyes looking at me.'

Michael won his commission, and the brigade tie was much in evidence during his time as secretary of state for defence. But politics came to the rescue. He applied to his commanding offer for permission to contest the Gower constituency in the Conservative interest in time for the October 1959 election. It was granted. He fought and predictably lost, for Gower's constituents were not all English spoken or 'respectable' like the Heseltines; and the Guards decided to dispense with his services. Heseltine, who had been keeping a close eye on his business while defending the realm, returned to West London to take up where he had left off.

The Heseltine/Labovitch publishing 'empire' was to boast three capital ships: *Town*, *Topic* and *Management Today*. The first two sank; the third is afloat today. There were, besides these three magazines, a flotilla of trade magazines each one of which made money. However well-produced they may have been, Michael had no wish to be known as the publisher of *Camera World* or *Cage Birds*; still, there are few draughts quite as heady as publishing, especially newspapers and magazines, and Heseltine saw success in the world of print as more reputable than success in property. Despite the evidence to the contrary, both before and since, publishing was considered to be, as is the wine trade, a gentleman's occupation.

Thus, in the Macmillan years Michael pursued a career in the three Ps: property, publishing and politics. Of the three, politics was the least important. He joined the Bow Group, a body of youngish Tory intellectuals, led by the likes of Geoffrey Howe and David Windlesham, but did not strive for office. It was enough for him to be associated with it. And the Bow Group, which in those days was on the left of the party, attracted more than its share of press attention. He did manage to get himself adopted as candidate for Coventry South, a Labour seat held by the prominent backbencher, the novelist Maurice Edelman. The seat was not winnable, not least because the swing would be against the Conservatives after what Labour had called, with a flair for publicity which was to desert it in office, 'the thirteen wasted years'. Nevertheless, it was good practice, and Michael flogged himself and his Jaguar (the chauffeur had fallen victim to economy) up and down the newly opened M1, passing several times a week under the Lego-like bridge which to this day faintly carries the legend 'Marples Must Go'.

In the early 'sixties Coventry was a boom town, but one which generally remained loyal to Labour. It was also a nursery for rising young Conservatives. In 1959 John Biffin had fought Richard Crossman and lost in Coventry North; now Michael was to do the same against Edelman. But he demonstrated his commitment and his radicalism. He had, on one occasion, the idea of running a series of advertisements in local newspapers owned by Woodrow Wyatt. The idea was to show, and printed in full colour, several electors who would be voting for Michael. One was a black bus conductor. His constituency agent was appalled; but Michael told him if the picture of the bus conductor came out, the association would have to find itself a new candidate.

Michael's loyalty to friends or to an ideal is one of his pleasing characteristics. In Tory terms he is left-wing, in that he is free of racial and class prejudice. No one whose political hero is David Lloyd George could be anything but impatient with the crustier, more selfish Conservatives whose well-developed sense of self-interest is all too often wrapped in the national flag. He is no humbug. His friendship for Tony Howard was demonstrated when Lord Hailsham threatened to sue Howard for a piece in *Town* magazine. At a meeting between Heseltine, Howard and the solicitor Peter Carter-Ruck, the latter suggested that Howard would do well to find his own lawyer. Michael was 'steady on parade'; the idea was dismissed and Howard was not left to fend on his own. In the event, the action was not pressed.

In 1961 Heseltine and Labovitch bought *Man about Town*, an obscure trade magazine dealing in men's clothes, a sort of rag trade gazette. They decided to turn it into a glossy, *Lilliput*-style monthly magazine which would appeal to the new affluent younger men who were to be found in London in particular. Clothes were banished to the back of the book, the front and middle being taken up with feature material of the sort now to be found in Mark Boxer's *Tatler* or in any of the Sunday newspaper magazines. The arts would also be covered.

Girls were to prove a problem for the new venture. Soft porn, as typified by magazines like *Mayfair* and *Penthouse*, was ten years away, and although *Lilliput* and *London Opinion* had carried photographs of nudes since before the war, the pictures left practically everything to the imagination. Michael and Clive decided to print soft focus pictures of pretty girls with their clothes on. Six years later when I became editor, and the sales of the magazine were falling, we discussed using pictures of naked women. Michael refused. He did so for two reasons: a native Welsh prudery, which

26

coexisted with a healthy love life; and the fear of giving offence. In 1965, at his adoption meeting as candidate for Tavistock, a safe seat, a constituent had brandished a cover of *Town* on which was a picture of a pretty girl, far from naked. Michael was accused of being a pornographer.

Clive Labovitch was the first editor of the magazine. He was succeeded by David Hughes, Nicholas Tomalin, Ron Bryden, Dick Adler, myself and finally, for three terminal weeks, Brian Moynihan. Over seven years the magazine did a Wedgwood Benn. Its title shrank, as a means of promotion, from *Man About Town* to *About Town* to *Town*. But the content was never as good as the layout and design. *Town* looked good, and its pictorial quality was, in large part, due to the skills of Tom Wolsley, the first art editor. Wolsley moonlighted from his job in an advertising agency for some months before joining *Town* full time.

The magazine had its early successes, but it was undercapitalised. Anthony Howard wrote a famous piece attacking the lobby correspondents, and another issue was devoted to Macmillan's Conservative Party. Well-known journalists on its staff included Ron Hall, later to edit *The Sunday Times* colour supplement and the *Sunday Express* magazine, Clive Irving and Michael Parkinson. I published Jill Tweedie's first piece and patronised a younger Jeffrey Bernard.

Town glittered for a time, briefly reaching a monthly circulation of some fifty thousand copies. It was very much a child of the 'swinging 'sixties', which Michael Heseltine most certainly was not. It managed to catch the hedonistic mood of the period, the age of Twiggy, Julie Christie, Catherine Deneuve and her sister Françoise Dorléac, Jack Profumo and George Wigg. The first Wilson slump killed it. Michael told me once that the magazine had, over seven years, 'never made a penny'. There was an echo when, twenty years later, the magazine was the star of an exhibition held in the Mall of ' 'Sixties Magazines'.

In 1962 Labovitch and Heseltine acquired a news magazine called *Topic*, once the property of a man who had made money leasing pigs. A profitable national news magazine on the lines of *Time* and *Newsweek* has been the intermittent ambition of several publishers. Most recently, Sir James Goldsmith launched *Now* only to lose a small fortune. Heseltine tried to do as much with far smaller resources. The project was doomed to be a costly failure.

Topic lasted four months, collapsing finally, heavy in debt, in December 1962. Its demise confirmed (as did the failure of *Now* twenty years later) the conventional wisdom which argued that in Britain, with the sale of fifteen million national newspapers a day (twelve million on Sunday), the intensive news coverage on television, there was no hope for a weekly news magazine on the American pattern. Nicholas Tomalin, then editing *Town*, was pulled across to work his magic on *Topic*; but to no avail. The magazine was not poorly written or produced, it was, in fact, rather better than *Now*; but its purchase was an alarming error of judgement on Heseltine and Labovitch's part. Heseltine sought desperately to find backers prepared to throw good money after bad, including the Carrs who owned the *News of the World*, but failed to find any.

This crisis coincided with a slump in the property market. Michael, who had built an estate of modernistic houses on the outskirts of Tenterden in Kent which had failed to sell, was doubly hit. He was reduced to putting himself at the mercy of his bank manager.

Heseltine was overwhelmed by debts amounting to a quarter of a million pounds, debts that derived in part from his unsold houses at Tenterden and in part from *Topic*. He later told Susan Barnes, in a profile of him published by *The Sunday Times* in 1983: 'As a shareholder I had limited liability, and the general manager of the bank concerned advised me to put several companies into liquidation. I said, "I'm sorry, I got these companies into that mess; I'll see it through." I thought that people who had done business with me would never believe it was right for me to go into public life if I had let a company with which I had been associated go under. "All right," said the bank, "it's on your shoulders." '

The crisis peaked on 21 December 1962. Heseltine went to his bank manager and explained the seriousness of his position. At the question 'What have you got?', Heseltine handed in his shares, the deeds on his house, the keys of his car, his gold watch. The manager gave him the money. He retired on the same day. 'That man,' said Heseltine, 'saved my career. I wrote to him several times later, but I never saw him again.'

It took the better part of ten years to get the debts under control. As he explained to Susan Barnes, 'For a time there were three categories of creditors: those who sent solicitors' letters, those who just issued writs and those whose writs were about to expire. You can guess which of the three we paid. If you do that every week, and survive, you remember the lessons. All the people now running Haymarket went through that experience with me. I would never have got through it without them. It creates a bond. Now it contributes to the excitement and the pride. It didn't seem like that at the time.'

In 1983 my wife and I were surprised to receive an invitation to a party at Thenford House to celebrate Michael's fiftieth birthday. The Palladian house, which he had bought in the late 'seventies from a one-time Tory MP for £750,000, together with a four-hundred-acre farm, was *en fête*. The park gates had been recast so as to include the initials in the metal work 'MRDH'. The guests were drawn from four decades of Michael's life: childhood friends from Gower; Oxford contemporaries; employees who had been tempered in the fire of the 'sixties, and prominent politicians and journalists. In the absence of the Howes, Heather and I occupied the 'bridal suite'; we had feared we might be put up at a temperance hotel in Banbury. Dinner took place at separate tables, clustered under the cupola of the great hall. I sat next to the wives of his doctor and his accountant, handsome women whose lips were sealed. At one stage I said that I remembered the lad when he lived in a detached house up the Gower Road in Swansea. 'That's nothing,' said his former secretary who was also at the table; 'I remember when the cheques went out with only one signature.'

The escape from bankruptcy, though narrow, saved Michael's political career. Even assuming that he would have gained his discharge, the stigma of having gone bust would have made a political career in the Tory Party out of the question. His determination to pay back the money owed, however long it took, is proof of his courage, and the force of his ambition. Clive Labovitch denies ever having said that 'Michael was the only gentile his Jewish friends were chary of doing business with', but the story has passed into legend. There is no doubt that Heseltine is a formidable operator. Labovitch, who parted company amicably enough with Michael in 1965, taking Cornmarket and the *Directories* (leaving Michael with Haymarket and the magazines), remains an admirer to this day. 'Michael is a very able businessman. He's got the judgement, is tough and a good negotiator. Very strong nerve.' What those who have worked closest with Michael will assert is Heseltine's honesty and straightforwardness. Lindsay Masters of Haymarket, who has played the Costa Gratsos to Heseltine's Aristotle Onassis, says, 'He is totally a man of his word. You don't have to write anything down with him.'

Haymarket's return to prosperity was helped greatly by the acquisition in 1964 of *Management Today*. It so happened that the British Institute of Management had a dullish journal it wished to improve. A consortium consisting of the *Economist*, *The Financial Times* and Haymarket was formed in competition against Thomson's. Clive and Brian Moynihan produced a dummy issue, with pictures and proper copy, in a fortnight flat and won the contract. Robert Heller was hired as editor, a post which he held with marked success until 1986. But the parting was a friendly one, although it would be difficult to avoid the conclusion that Michael got the better deal. *Management Today* was among the maga-

zines which fell to Haymarket Press, and it was not long
before Michael bought out both the *Financial Times* and the
Economist.

I saw a good deal of Michael during the early 'sixties. I was
married, living in Blackheath and sitting in the House,
writing, in my spare time, a column for Brian Inglis's
Spectator. I had never been engaged in business with
Michael. Two events we shared at that time stand out in my
memory. On 12 August 1961 we travelled to West Berlin at
the invitation of the Atlantic Association of Young Political
Leaders. We spent the Saturday touring the divided city,
admiring Queen Nefertiti, and inspecting the refugee camps
set up in West Berlin for Germans fleeing from the East. We
woke the next morning to discover that the East Germans
had built the wall. The British garrison put a car and driver at
our disposal and we drove into East Berlin to watch the
Communists sealing off their quarter of the city. Soviet tanks
were linked up beneath the trees on avenues leading towards
the Western sectors. Later we walked on the Western side of
the Brandenburg Gate in the gap between a crowd of angry
West Berliners held back by the police, and a line of Vopos.
We were soaked by the water cannons of East and West. It
was an introduction of sorts to the Cold War. Later, in the
'eighties, when Michael was secretary of state for defence
with the task of getting the better of the Campaign for
Nuclear Disarmament, he went back to Berlin to make a
speech denouncing the disarmers.

In 1962, after a tempestuous courtship, Michael married
Anne Williams, the daughter of a Welsh solicitor. I was
invited to be best man. As he had been mine in 1955 when I
married Paula Baron at the Caxton Hall, it was in the nature
of a return match. The reception was held at the Savoy and
the guests included many a political rising hope. In my speech
I drew attention to Anne's legs which, I said, would be an
asset on many a political platform. Michael replied in kind.
Elspeth Howe, the wife of Geoffrey Howe, who was standing

behind a curtain, was heard to observe, 'What a couple of shits.' She could well have been right.

Having failed to win Coventry South from Maurice Edelman in October 1964, Heseltine was lucky enough to be adopted to succeed Sir Henry Studholme as Conservative candidate for Tavistock, in Devon. In seven years he had climbed from hopeless seat to marginal, and then to inherit a safe one; a satisfactory if unremarkable progress. Studholme was very much a traditional Tory member, a knight of the shires, a weight in the upper-class ballast that for so many years had served to keep the party on an even keel. The burghers of Tavistock and its environs did not quite know what to make of his colourful replacement.

Tall, good-looking and sharply dressed (he was no longer buying his suits from Darley Mills), Michael took with him to the comfortably-off of Devon who − almost to a man and more particular a woman − made up the constituency party selection committee, a dazzling, if indistinct, metropolitan reputation. His party credentials were fine. He had been president of the Oxford Union, he had clearly made money. That he should be a publisher of glossy magazines of the sort which had nothing in common with *Country Life* could be attributed to a youthful exuberance. While not out of the topmost drawer, he did, in Michael's own words at the time, 'pass as white'. At the 1966 general election he duly came into his inheritance. He was elected Member of Parliament for Tavistock in the Conservative interest, and has sat in the Commons ever since.

Michael Heseltine had timed his arrival well. After the twin defeats of 1964 and '66, the Tories had lost a hundred MPs, not all of whom were dead wood. The rump, under Ted Heath, the party's new leader, was determined to oppose Wilsonian socialism with all the means at its disposal. The young Heseltine, still in his middle thirties, was not the man to miss chances. By now he was a confident speaker, almost without nerves. He did not suffer from a complaint to which many are prone: the debilitating tendency to see both sides of any question. And there is everything to be said for entering parliament in opposition.

In government the newly elected backbencher is expected to hold his fire. His opponents are fair game, but he would be rash if, growing impatient for promotion, he were tempted to rock the boat. What the whips are looking for is his vote not his voice. The ambitious MP, looking to place his foot on the first step of the ladder, should vote when required to do so and, if possible, make his mark defending his colleagues upstairs on committee. From the beginning Michael took care not to join in the endless and often exciting disputes which rend friend from friend; his fire was directed across the Chamber.

What were the qualities he brought to the party? Most Tory MPs are not clever; it is enough that they are 'sound'. While no intellectual, Heseltine was bright for a Conservative, and blessed with high horsepower. He applied himself to the task of making the kind of name that would appeal to the party whips, those not-so-secret members of the party's secret police whose job is not only to see that the government gets its business through the House, but to spot for talent. Not even the most obtuse member of the Tory whips office could have overlooked the Member for Tavistock. Never a clubbable man, Heseltine took care to make one friend who was to stand him in good stead: Peter Walker.

I had won my seat, Rochester, in October 1959 by a thousand votes. I stood again in 1966 and lost by two thousand. By that April I was out of work and between marriages. Michael offered me the editorship of *Town* which I was pleased to accept. Anthony Howard, who had been offered it on many previous occasions, had always refused. He was wiser than I. Michael promptly sacked Dick Adler, the editor, and put me in his chair at a salary of three thousand pounds. I brought out twelve issues before I, too, was discharged.

In the year I worked for Michael, we lived in the same house in Chepstow Villas, Notting Hill Gate. Michael and

Anne had the basement and the first two floors, Heather and I the top floor flat. It was not a happy arrangement. Michael and I could get along fine, but the four of us were incompatible. *Town*'s circulation continued to fall; the budget for contributors was cut each month, and it was not long before I was reduced to using copy commissioned, but not used, by my predecessors. Relations between Michael and me grew distant. There was a moment of light relief, when the neighbours complained about Anne Heseltine having had the outside of the house painted shocking pink. 'People will think the blacks have moved in,' they said.

In April 1967, having done his best, if always at second-hand, to make life difficult for me, Michael finally sacked me giving me a month's salary. We were obliged to sell the top floor back to him at the price we paid for it. Our friendship was over.

The episode is unimportant save for the light it sheds upon Michael. It has been said that he does tend to pick his friends for what they can contribute to him, and once they have done so, the friendship is expendable. That is Ian Josephs' view; his old partner was hurt not to have been invited to Michael's wedding. His friendship with Peter Walker, close at the start when Peter, much the senior of the two, had something to contribute, became less close as he was slowly overtaken. Yet they remain close allies. On the other hand, friendships wear out. Michael is not a social animal, a fact which Anne, galloping across the unkind Midlands in pursuit of the fox, may find disappointing. It does restrict his circle of acquaintance. I interviewed him in the mid 'seventies for a profile I was writing on him for the *Illustrated London News*. I asked him if he had ever made a mistake. 'Yes, sacking you,' was his surprising reply.

Trying It on For Size

Heseltine as politician has always been hard to ignore. He does look the part. US Senators are portrayed on the cinema either by Robert Redford (Joe Biden of Delaware) or by Charles Laughton (Chuck Mathias of Rhode Island) – good-looking idealists or dilapidated cynics. Congressmen and MPs are, more often than not, portrayed on film and television as middle-aged men on the make who betray their wives and neglect their constituents. In this country, politicians have enjoyed a bad press. Cecil Parkinson is better known for his love life than for the part he played in Mrs Thatcher's election victory in 1983, Jack Profumo put his stamp on the Macmillan years, while John Stonehouse might have sprung from the pen of Jeffrey Archer. Michael Heseltine has been happily free of scandal. His hair, his suits and his conference oratory have cast him in the role of Action Man.

He does tend to polarise opinions. In the late 'seventies he spoke in Aldershot at an all-day Tory women's conference. As he climbed on to the platform, a brigadier's widow whispered to me, 'Why doesn't he get his hair cut?' When he had made his speech, she hissed, 'Why is he not the leader of our great party?' As I left the House at the end of term in July 1986, I ran into Ted Heath. He asked me how I intended to spend the recess. I told him that I was going to write Michael Heseltine's biography. 'That won't take long,' was his reply. Cecil Parkinson, before the Fall, told me that whenever

Michael's name was mentioned in front of Margaret Thatcher, she would murmur through pursed lips, 'Michael is not one of us.' And, plainly, he was not.

Michael neglects the House of Commons. His public profile may be high, but his attendance in the smoking-room is an event to be remarked upon. Most MPs make for the tea-room immediately after Questions at 3.30 in the afternoon. We queue for tea and rock cakes of an alarming density. Labour MPs congregate at one end; Tories at the other. We are invariably joined by whips in plain clothes, passing themselves off as one of the lads. We gossip, glance at copies of the *Standard*, open our post. In the week after his resignation over Westland, Michael was seen to take tea. *We* knew *him*; to how many of his colleagues, especially those elected in 1983, he could put a name, is anyone's guess.

Michael Heseltine is not one of nature's backbenchers. After all he has been one for, at most, only five years. In the Wilson years he was for the greater part an Opposition frontbencher, working in the late 'sixties as part of Peter Walker's team, shadowing transport and Mrs Barbara Castle. Ted Heath made him parliamentary secretary for transport in June 1970, and Margaret Thatcher made him secretary of state for the environment and a privy councillor, in May 1979. Following Westland, Michael has had to discover how the other half of Westminster lives.

Although I have never been a minister of the crown, I can recognise the gulf that opens up between the leaders and the led. A minister spends a long day in his ministry, generally engaged upon a series of routine meetings, coping with delegations, worrying about Question Time and, on occasion, thinking about what next to do. Unlike backbenchers, ministers have no equivalent of the weekly meeting of the 1922 Committee, that 'parliament' of the skimmed milk, where Walder's Law reigns (the late David Walder, MP for Clitheroe, once stated that 'the first three people to speak at the '22, on any subject, are mad'). A minister will perform at Question Time approximately once every three weeks when the ministerial 'team' will sit on the bench together, taking it in turns to field the bowling. A speech from the despatch box is a rare event which usually passes without notice. Sometimes a minister will come into the House for lunch, but more often he will be lunching at someone else's expense at the Savoy. At the end of a day's work in the ministry, or in the country, if his diary so dictates, a minister will go over to the House at least until the vote at ten o'clock, sometimes for much longer. But he will take refuge in his room beneath the Chamber, emerging only when summoned by the division bell when for six minutes or more he is vulnerable to the importuning of his less distinguished colleagues.

There was always something splendid about Michael's isolation, a condition brought on in part by temperament and in part by pride. In a revealing response to Susan Barnes in his *Sunday Times* profile, from which I have already quoted, Michael said, 'I'm not a very clubbable person – sitting around with a drink and people coming up to you. That kind of getting-to-know-how-you-tick is a time-consuming exercise. I do have a considerable workload. Anyhow, I am what I am. And if I did change to suit other people, they would then regroup and find something else they didn't like – probably what I had created at their request. All my life, people have tried to change me. At the age of seven I was advised by a school prefect as to how I would do better if only I was different. I'm not sure where he is now.' When I told him that he would never get to the top unless he made friends, he said, 'Nonsense. Look at Ted and Margaret. They didn't have any friends, and they got to the top.' True enough; fortune played its part. Michael, however, will need all the friends he can muster if he is to get to the top.

A minister's isolation is not total. In recent years even the most obscure have been given parliamentary private secretaries, the PPSs, backbenchers who go into service in order to further their careers. The task of the PPS is to add tonic to his master's gin, help him on with his overcoat, and keep him informed. A minister can ask for someone specific to fill the post or, if he has no one in mind, the whips will find him someone. In Ted Heath's time Michael's PPS was John Stanley who rose – but did not fall – with him, and in Margaret's Keith Hampson, by whom he stood when Hampson was accused of soliciting in a gay bar (he was found not guilty), and then Nicholas Baker. A more substantial link with the backbenches is the party committee, the officers of which hold regular meetings with the secretary of state and his ministers. It was in my capacity as a vice-chairman of the party's defence committee that I was able to keep an eye on what was happening at the ministry of defence.

When I returned to the Commons as Member for Aldershot in 1970, resuming my career on the backbenches, Michael had, on the strength of his performance in Opposition, been promoted to the ministry of transport as a junior minister. He must have been somewhat disappointed at the relative lowliness of the position, as he had been the Opposition spokesman on the subject. But it is never easy to fit in the deserving, giving to each the post he merits, a task which in 1970 would have been carried out very largely by the chief whip, Francis Pym. In any event, Michael was quickly moved: first to the department of the environment, one of Ted Heath's 'monster ministries', housed in a hideous multi-block complex in Marsham Street underneath which are to be found deep atomic shelters, and then in 1972 he was made minister for aerospace.

Ministers at the department of the environment have their offices on the seventeenth floor, with panoramic views stretching northwards to the hills of Hampstead and to the Downs to the south. The sight of so much real estate was felt, in Michael's case anyway, to be bad for the character. He soon became very unpopular with his civil servants. Ministers are faced with a choice of sorts: they can swim with the tide or against it. No one who knew anything of Michael could have expected him to do what he was told.

In 1970, on becoming a junior minister, Michael refused to

be patronised by his civil servants. ' "Pussy", that's what they called us', he is quoted as saying. 'We were the scum of the earth, tolerated by the civil servants.' Tolerated, or not, he was soon strongly disliked. Heseltine has said, 'In my private office I had the nicest but totally inexperienced kids straight out of university. If they went along to a more senior civil servant and said, "My boss has asked if you will do this", they were told where to go. I blew my top. You're not going to use me to train your officials. I'm going to have more experienced civil servants to help me do my job. This is my private office. This was the phenomenon, a wilful junior minister who was going to do his job as he best believed it could be done. And I had the very, very, substantial support of Peter Walker (the secretary of state). I hope I never let him down.'

It was as minister for aerospace that Michael Heseltine first stumbled. He was accused, over the so-called Hovertrain incident, of lying to a Commons select committee, although there seemed no point in his doing so. He was obliged to come to the House and to explain that he had no intention of misleading the committee. Tom King, who was Michael's eventual successor as secretary of state at the department of the environment, says of the episode: 'It was either just a mistake or he was inadequately briefed. But because of his high profile, if anything happens to him the event becomes high profile, too. Ordinarily, the thing would not have warranted any real attention.' It was a storm got up in the Opposition's tea-cup which gave rise to his nickname 'Tarzan', which rivals 'Goldilocks' among the agnostic. Why 'Tarzan', I am not too clear. Michael is totally unathletic. Tarzan may however have its origins in a story once current that Heseltine strangled his dog with his bare hands. The truth is more mundane. His Alsatian attacked and killed a Siamese cat in Heseltine's Kensington drawing-room; Michael was obliged to restrain the dog, which was put down on the following day. 'Goldilocks' is not very clever either, as the three bears are difficult to identify. The Commons is an uncharitable place, many of whose members, including some Conservatives, distrusted his ambition and disapproved of his methods.

It would be enough for most politicians to reach the level of middle-ranking minister, a rank which Michael reached at aerospace at the age of thirty-nine. For many the road thereafter would be downhill; a period of hard work to be rewarded by a polite exchange of letters with the prime minister of the day, and membership of the Privy Council, a distinction which adds 'The Rt Hon.' to one's name. For Michael, it was a second step up the ladder which could have led, quite swiftly, had Ted Heath decided to go to the country a week earlier than he did in early 1974, to a cabinet post. In the event, the Prime Minister miscalculated, and the Tories, while winning more votes than Labour, ended up with fewer seats. It was obvious that Harold Wilson would repeat his manoeuvre of ten years previously. In 1964, elected to office with the slimmest of majorities, he had bided his time, went to the country eighteen months later and was handsomely rewarded. In February 1974, after the traumas of the 'three day week', all Wilson had to do was repeat the tactic. The Tories would be out of office for a parliament.

Defeat destroyed Ted and delayed Michael's progress. While Heath's enemies, led by Edward du Cann, the chairman of the '22, and members of his executive, conspired to bring about their leader's downfall, Michael Heseltine had to take stock. He was a Heath man, but he also had his way to make. What were the weapons at his disposal?

He had plenty of money. He had become the majority shareholder in a multimillion-pound Haymarket Press of which he had been, in Opposition, founder, chairman and managing director. He had sold the company to the British Printing Corporation in 1968, and in 1971, while a junior minister, had bought out BPC's 60% interest for one and a half million pounds. He was allotted 101,998 shares; and his wife, Anne, 18,002 shares for their six hundred thousand pounds majority shareholding. While a minister holds office, his or her shares are held in trust. Deprived of his ministry by electoral misfortune, Michael was not short of the odd bob. After fifteen years of running boarding houses, selling property and publishing magazines, good bad and indifferent, Michael had hit the jackpot.

The ambitious Conservative in Opposition has a hundred ways to make good. Colleagues have speakers to find for constituency functions: annual dinners, half-day conferences, Friday evening supper clubs. By 1974 Michael was already a crowd puller, the kind of visiting Tory of whom the *Daily Telegraph* reader would have formed a good opinion, a coming man who would sell tickets. There is a department at Tory Central Office that acts as broker between constituency agent and party speaker, and Michael has been among the three or four speakers most in demand for the last twelve years. Even today, after Westland, he has kept his rating. But MPs are particularly vulnerable to the importuning colleague, the implication being that one good turn merits another. In return for Michael's appearance in Aldershot, I addressed the women of Henley. Blessed with stamina, Michael was able to do his friends a favour at the same time as impressing the party faithful and, by the publication of a press release, get his name in the national and local newspapers. The price might well have been tedium, indigestion and fatigue, but he plainly thought and thinks it worth it.

Some ambitious Tories, anxious to cultivate a reputation for brains in a party which is not overendowed with them, put pen to paper. A pamphlet on the future of rates for the Conservative Political Centre; a chapter in a concoction published by the International Institute for Strategic Studies, or by Chatham House; a rare turnover article in *The Times* – all or any of these could add gravitas, but Michael is no writer. There are those who might add that he cannot read either, but that would be the uncharitableness of the Smoking-Room. Michael is mildly dyslexic, a fashionable condition to be found among middle-class children whose

mothers drive yellow Volvos and belong to the Social Democrats. But reading difficulties are real enough, and Michael,
both at Oxford and in Whitehall, has had to rely on
judiciously arranged note-taking and upon graphs of one
kind and another. His dyslexia was diagnosed at second-
hand by my father, the neurologist, Dr Macdonald Critchley,
to whom Michael sent his son Rupert. Having seen the tests
and the prognosis, Michael decided that he, too, suffered
from the disability. The condition has not been so severe as to
prevent Heseltine from writing at all, only to discourage him
from doing so.

In Opposition, the best way to get one's name in the papers is
to attack the other side, and, as we have seen, Michael has
always been sensible enough to resist temptation and direct
his fire away from his colleagues. In 1976 he became famous.
The cause of this was the episode of the mace.

The occasion was a debate on the second reading of the bill
to nationalise the shipbuilding and aircraft industries. I sat
directly behind the Opposition front bench for the wind-up,
which took place between nine and ten o'clock, so I had a
ringside seat. The House had been much exercised by the
bill's alleged hybridity, a technical term for a flaw discovered
by Robert Maxwell-Hyslop, a Tory MP who had been an
enemy of Michael's at Oxford. Passions ran high. The
Labour government's majority was either one, two or three,
depending on whether or not the Irish bothered to turn up,
and the excitement was intense as Michael Heseltine and
Michael Foot, arguably the best debaters in the House,
divided the final hour between them. MPs, who are obliged
by the nature of things to endure 'hours and hours of
exquisite boredom' (the quotation belongs to Aneurin
Bevan), take the trouble to dine well, quitting their tables
only as the name of the Opposition's front bench speaker
flashes upon the television monitor screens. This time it was
going to be too good to miss.

I forget what was said, no doubt it was all predictable

enough; but when the vote was called upon our amendment, the whips responsible for counting the votes jostled for position in front of the speaker's chair. As the winning side invariably takes the right-hand position, the sight of two Opposition whips and two government whips jostling for the right-hand side clearly meant that the result had been a tie. At this the Tory benches erupted with sound. A tie would mean that the speaker would traditionally award his casting vote to the government, but, were the second vote on the original motion to be tied, then the speaker would be compelled to vote, by precedent, in favour of the Opposition. The government looked in peril of losing a vitally important piece of legislation, and a general election could well result from it – an election which, given the Callaghan government's unpopularity (Harold Wilson had surprisingly retired earlier that year), would be likely to be won by the Tories. The noise was deafening; the excitement acute.

In the event, the government won the second division by one vote, seemingly plucked out of the air. The word went round the Tory benches that the government chief whip, Michael Cocks, had persuaded one of his flock to break his pair – that is, his private agreement with a member of the other side not to vote. Life at Westminster without a regular 'pair' would be purgatory indeed. The fact that this charge turned out to be quite untrue, was neither here nor there. We Tories, deprived at the last moment of our kill, were ready to believe anything.

We howled with frustration and yelled 'cheat'. Some Labour MPs started singing 'The Red Flag', the first time that dirge had been heard in the Chamber since the great days of 1945. The House of Commons was on its feet. It was at this juncture that Michael Heseltine, standing in his place opposite the despatch box, seized the mace, symbol of parliamentary rectitude, and advanced upon the government front bench. Whether he meant to present it to Michael Foot as a prettily ironic gesture, or to clout him, or Callaghan, over the head with it, has become the stuff of legend. Whatever

Heseltine's intention, Jim Prior was too quick for him. He moved swiftly behind him and took away the mace, replacing it in its customary position but the wrong way round.

Immediately, pandemonium broke out. Punches were thrown. I moved with others to put myself *à la* Lytton Strachey between Michael and the cohorts of the Left, including Tom Swain, a bruiser the worse for drink. Missing Michael, Swain struck the youthful Anthony Nelson, one of our party's 'sixteen-year-old merchant bankers'. Geoffrey Rippon, purple with rage, lashed out at the choristers with his rolled-up order paper, while the serjeant at arms, a crusty retired rear admiral, used 'nautical language' (in the decorous words of *The Times*) in an attempt to dampen down the fires. After it was all over, Michael stood quivering with passion in the members' lobby.

The great men and women of our party were furious. Willie Whitelaw trumpeted his annoyance. It seemed to them that the publicity which resulted from Michael's frustrated attempt at what looked like being assault, if not battery, had distracted attention from the sins, real and imaginary, of the Labour government. And it showed a sad lack of self-control. I suspect that Michael went to bed alarmed and chastened, but, as he told me a day or so later, he soon changed his mind. It appeared that he could not put his face out of doors without being congratulated by hoi polloi. The Tory Party activists in particular applauded so virile an example of opposition. He had become the hero of the Right. If it is necessary in politics to possess both passion and vulgarity – in its proper sense, that is – Michael had demonstrated that he had both qualities, even to excess. He was to show something of the same ten years later in the cabinet room at No. 10 Downing Street.

At the time of the Peasants' Revolt which led to Margaret Thatcher's election as party leader in 1975, Michael stayed on the side of the barons. His loyalty was to Ted Heath whom he had served faithfully in government. Heath had made many enemies in the ten years of his leadership: he had led the party, despite being 'Selsdon Man', from left of centre; and he had conspicuously failed to practise the political arts. His parsimony when it came to handing out the twice-yearly honours to clapped-out MPs was bitterly resented by those who sought consolation of a sort. He was also reluctant to flatter the simple. Most important of all, he had led the party to defeat in three of the four elections it had fought under his leadership. Shocked by February 1974, and humiliated by October, many Tory MPs were only too ready to use the electoral machinery, bequeathed to them by the maverick Tory MP Humphrey Berkeley, to rid themselves of a man they saw as a political albatross. We Tories can be an unattractive lot.

While some of the more moderately inclined Tories thought that Ted should go, the main opposition to him came from the party's right wing, the 51% of the Tory Party that had been unable to exercise a controlling influence since the days of Neville Chamberlain. In the first of the two elections for the party leadership which were held in 1975, Michael Heseltine voted first for Heath and then, in the second vote, for Willie Whitelaw. It is worth looking again at the figures of the first of the two votes, the one which forced Heath out of the contest. They were: Margaret Thatcher 130; Heath 119; and Hugh Fraser 16, a Thatcher majority of only eleven, five less than the votes cast for Fraser, a splendid man but a no-hope candidate. It was, given the circumstances, a close-run thing; but, having defeated the party leader, the Thatcher bandwagon was able to pick up momentum.

Why was Michael not tempted to vote for Mrs Thatcher? It was no secret that he was no lover of 'petticoat government', and Margaret's sex may have played a part. Michael is nothing if not conventional. He had had little or nothing to do with her; there would have been nothing whatever in common between them. Politicians have a small circle of friends, a wider one of acquaintances, and a third ring made up of more or less total strangers. Margaret would have been in Michael's third division. She had also acquired the reputation of being a fundamentalist of a kind rarely found among the more sophisticated Tories; she seemed to share the views so often expressed by party workers, and what was worse, to be prepared to articulate them. Michael had been brought up to believe that the duty of a Conservative MP was to moderate, not to amplify, the views of his supporters. They were, in short, chalk and cheese.

After the party's defeat in February 1974, Ted Heath had made Michael the party's spokesman on trade and industry, a major promotion for him. Labour's plans to nationalise and to tax British industry would put Heseltine in the forefront of the party battle. Margaret's victory would serve to reshuffle the pack. In the event trade and industry went to her mentor Sir Keith Joseph (once described by Harold Macmillan as 'the only boring Jew I have ever met'), while Michael was given the environment. It was not what he wanted but he took it nonetheless.

It was in 1975 that Michael Heseltine discovered the Conservative Party conference. This annual jamboree, held at a seaside resort out of season, had been invented in the 1880s as part of the process of bringing parliamentary democracy to the people. He had, as an aspirant, visited Blackpool and Brighton, one of five thousand or so representatives (Tories are never 'delegated' to attend) anxious to rub shoulders with the great and, if possible, to speak for five minutes or so from the rostrum. To deliver a minor conference speech was the ambition of every prominent Young Conservative. Such an opportunity had been the springboard for a bevy of Heseltine's contemporaries: William Van Straubenzee, Peter Walker (later to become the YC national chairman), Nicholas Scott, Kenneth Warren and Andrew Bowden. But Michael was not one of nature's Young Conservatives. He did not go to the conference to make his name from the floor; he made it from the platform.

Tories gather at the seaside to rally rather than to confer. The party conference is an exercise in political public relations, its purpose to put the party, in or out of government, in the best possible light. To this end the proceedings are discreetly rigged. The chairman of the conference, who is, more often than not, a genial old buffer with short sight, is guided by senior party functionaries as to his choice of speaker. The motions for debate are carefully chosen in Smith Square, and dissent, if the representatives are so ill-mannered as to show it, strictly rationed. If my description appears an unduly cynical one, I hasten to add that I would prefer the conference to be rigged. No less a man than A.J. Balfour said that he would sooner take advice from his valet than from a Conservative conference.

Only a small minority of the faithful come to make trouble. Most give up part of their holidays to enjoy themselves, and if that means listening to speeches, the content of which they largely agree with, then so be it. Recently there has grown up a conference 'fringe' in imitation of our political opponents, where the more vital can plead and posture to their hearts' content. But the conference itself, which lasts for four days, is both a sounding board and a litmus paper. It is orchestrated so that the climax comes on the Friday afternoon with the address of the party leader, an event which, in recent years, has been used by Mrs Thatcher to tell the nation to pull up its socks. On each of the other days, ministers or shadow ministers respond to debates on their own subjects. Before 1975 the platform speakers, with rare exceptions like Iain Macleod, generally kept things dull, and the applause was dutiful and restrained. Today every minister is given a standing ovation, a tiresome new custom for which many blame Michael Heseltine's exuberant oratory.

Oratory has rarely been a Tory failing, particularly at conferences. Sir Winston Churchill, who used to fly into Lytham St Anne's like the Lord God of Hosts for the final rally, would read a prepared speech. Anthony Eden was as bland as a pot of yoghurt, Harold Macmillan ill at ease, Sir Alec would address the conference as if it were a county agricultural show, and Ted Heath, a City board meeting.

Margaret is didactic and often boring. I have already made an exception for Iain Macleod who could speak superbly; so, too, could Quintin Hailsham and Lord Hill, but by and large Conservatives do not bother to remove their silver spoons. A glance at Michael Heseltine's rivals will reinforce my point. As speakers they are at best competent (Peter Walker, Kenneth Baker) and at worst plain dull (Patrick Jenkin, Leon Brittan). Called upon in 1975 to reply from the platform to the debate on the environment, Michael tossed a handful of salt into the stew.

He took the hall by storm. He claims to spend a year on his conference speeches; pardonable hyperbole. Nevertheless, he takes trouble with them. Instead of sticking to his environmental brief, Heseltine had the chutzpah to stray into the more congenial territory of his peers. A polite reference to several laboured speeches from the floor, an obligatory nod in favour of local government reform and the future of the rates, and he was off into the wide Blue yonder. Unused to passion and inured to vulgarity, five thousand sleepy members of the middle class – it is only in more recent years that the party conference has become a largely working-class festival – woke to the realisation that here was something special. Having hijacked politics, as it were, Michael could range uninterrupted over the field of battle, choosing his targets at will. His colleagues seated on the platform, each one with a speech to make, were startled into paying attention. Some thought that Michael had gone over the top. Willie Whitelaw, his thunder stolen, exploded with rage. Others took refuge in pique. 'Heseltine may have the looks of Adonis,' said one frontbencher, 'but he has a mind like Hampstead Garden Suburb.' The television cameras were forced to overrun, and Michael, his mane in studied disarray, sat down to what was then a most extraordinary occurrence for a party conference, a standing ovation.

Since October 1975 the Heseltine conference speech has become a highlight of the occasion, a performance designed to put his rivals in the shade and Michael in the public prints.

Senior Tories, anxious to keep their thunder, have encouraged the BBC to quit Blackpool at the first sign of a Heseltine peroration in favour of 'Listen with Mother'. Political journalists equipped themselves with stop watches to time the inevitable ovation, and his friends, unwilling to come to terms with the phenomenon, damned his demagoguery with faint praise: 'Clint Eastwood playing Mussolini.' Yet, however cynical the response might have been, his colleagues and the political commentators saluted his idealism. Michael's prejudices were not those of his audience. He was the sole Tory, in or out of office, who was capable of taking the party activist by the scruff of the neck and showing her the real world outside. His compassion, in a party which was being encouraged to discount it, was self-evident. Who other than Michael in the Tory Party has dared draw attention to the plight of the unemployed, or has spoken in favour of more money for the inner cities? Not only has he dared – but to have been applauded for doing so! Heseltine's technique was to establish first of all his anti-socialist credentials. The enemy would be ridiculed and then 'destroyed': having done this, it was time for home truths. In the 'eighties his performance came to be rivalled by Norman Tebbit's. Tebbit is no formal orator, but he does have an attractively self-deprecating style and a pretty wit. He also has the undoubted advantage of prejudices shared by his audience. The two are well-matched. Michael could get the conference to its feet; Tebbit could put it on its knees.

Thus, at the end of the 'seventies Heseltine had it made. Rich enough to run three houses – one in Nettlebed, another in Belgravia and a third on Exmoor – he was the boss of a flourishing business. His flair had made him the favourite of the party worker, and his application had placed him among the leaders of the Conservative Party. He was being talked about as a future prime minister. Office, when it came, could only be among the highest in the land. He was only forty-six. What has gone wrong?

Lord of All He Surveyed

On the fourth of May 1979, a few weeks past his forty-sixth birthday, Michael Heseltine was invited by the Prime Minister to join her cabinet. To rise to the rank of cabinet minister is no mean feat, and there were commentators who wondered during the election campaign whether Michael would, in the event of a Conservative victory, be so rewarded. Cynics recalled that in 1975, when Margaret Thatcher became leader, his place in the shadow cabinet had been saved only by the good fortune of being due to speak at the quarterly meeting of the party's Central Council alongside his brand-new leader. In the event, four years on, the invitation came by telephone on the Friday morning after polling day. He was offered the environment.

Margaret and Michael were still not close. The Prime Minister owed him no favours. However, she could not fail to recognise his pre-eminence among leading Tories. Had he not galvanised the party conference on four successive years, to say nothing of the episode of the mace? She also recognised his talents, and not least of these was his managerial ability. He had never joined the Institute of Economic Affairs, nor sat at the feet of Sir Keith Joseph at his most beguiling. But he was one Tory who could run a whelk stall.

The gossip in the strangers' dining-room was that Heseltine had sulked for twenty-four hours after accepting the offer. There may have been something in it. Elation may well have given way to dismay. Environment was way down the cabinet pecking order, and the implication was that he would be excluded from membership of those cabinet committees which really mattered, the economic ones. Mrs Thatcher, who had inherited Ted Heath's shadow cabinet, had little choice but to include its members in her first cabinet. (She refused to include Heath, who might well have expected to become foreign secretary, but offered him the embassy in Washington instead. It was quite properly refused.) But all cabinets consist of concentric circles: in Heath's Margaret had been cast into outer darkness, her views unsought; in Margaret's, Michael was to be kept away from treasury matters, the preserve of the 'true believer'.

Nevertheless Michael is not the sort to fluff his chances. However disappointed he might have been, the future held promise. He felt that he could guide the affairs of a great department of state to a position of hitherto unknown importance. The cellars of Marsham Street were too deep for dancing, but its four towers were as topless as those of Troy.

What luggage did Michael bring with him to the department of the environment? He had flair, but had he judgement? Looking back to the mace, there were many who thought not. He could speak well, better from a platform than in the House. He had the necessary stamina, and no one doubted his ambition. But in what did he believe?

Many would say 'in himself'. Senior politicians with a role to play in Opposition, and Michael had shadowed Peter Shore at the department of the environment, come to believe their speeches. Heseltine's rhetoric was predictable enough: it included the 'seventies concerns so popular with the Conservative research department; the alarming growth of the bureaucratic state; the belief that there were too many constraints on the wealth creators; concern about culpable neglect of the private sector; about the dictatorship of unrepresentative union bosses and the stifling effect of high taxation.

Mrs Thatcher put it thus: 'We all wanted strong defence, more resources for law and order, lower taxation, more private enterprise, less government control. Aiming in that general direction we were all conviction politicians.' As we shall see, Heseltine's convictions were not necessarily Thatcher's, and there was one other fundamentally important difference. Mrs Thatcher's Methodist upbringing in the corner shop in Grantham apparently left her with a degree of impatience with those who are not so well equipped to rise above their disadvantages. His compassion may be sentimental in origin, borrowed from his hero Lloyd George, but it is genuine nonetheless. In fact, Michael's concern for the plight of the inner cities and their disadvantaged inhabitants predates the riots of the summer of 1981. Michael Heseltine is hard to label, but he is closer to the 'Tory Democrats' than he is to the newer Conservatives who model their philosophy on Richard Cobden and Samuel Smiles.

The civil servants at the department of the environment awaited Heseltine's arrival with some apprehension. Many remembered the brash young man of 1970 who would not take a murmured 'no' for an answer. They feared he would prove to be exceedingly difficult to work with. The fit of bad temper he had shown in refusing to work with inexperienced civil servants was not completely forgotten. Nor was the fact that he had got his way.

In so far as this anxiety still lingered, it quickly proved false. Heseltine had matured. His closest advisors during his time as secretary of state know of no instance when he ever lost his cool, despite the fact that for most of the period he was working under great pressure. The view today is that Heseltine proved a hard but fair taskmaster, quick to forgive mistakes, although he did not expect an official to make the same error twice. They very seldom did. Equally he lost little time in lavishing praise for a job well done. He put his civil servants at their ease and was soon felt to be one of the least pompous ministers they had ever served.

Those who believed that he would run the department like an autocrat were also to be disappointed. In reality, the reverse proved to be the case. He insisted that most of the work on major issues was dealt with by a member of his ministerial team. Tom King and John Stanley, who had been his PPSs in Opposition, were quickly given a chance to prove their worth as ministers of state. Heseltine took the longer view, took care to be well informed, and avoided needless interference in other people's jobs.

There were other civil servants who, having read about Michael in the newspapers and watched him perform against their team from the box in the House (a minister is supported on the floor of the House by a small group of his officials who sit ready to scribble notes of fact or encouragement), thought him to be superficial and none too bright. Superficial he may be, but any doubts about his intelligence could be laid at the door of his reading difficulties.

In order to cope with his dyslexia, Heseltine required his staff to prepare a brief memo listing all the salient points on an issue. Although he reads slowly, his ability to memorise what he sees on paper is excellent. On the basis of these notes, he would call in a large group, usually around twelve, comprising his ministerial colleagues and their senior civil servants. He would listen to both groups with equal attention, and to the middle-ranking civil servants as much as to senior bureaucrats. He would arrive at decisions in this way, having exchanged ideas and information among the group. Although, as might be expected from his lack of reading background, he did not always know a lot of the detail, his perception of the essential points involved in an issue was acute. It is the view of those who served him that Heseltine is perfectly able to hold his own with any of his departmental officials.

Thus Heseltine was soon to command the respect of his civil servants. Over time he won the ungrudging loyalty of many of them. And he did so in spite of a desire to prune his ministry. Some were equivocal: on the one hand, Heseltine was perceived to have admirable qualities and a likeable personality; on the other, one of his objectives was to instill in his officials a managerial, cost-cutting approach which did not rule out redundancy, a policy which could not fail to be unpopular.

Nevertheless, despite his zeal, Heseltine did engender a remarkable degree of loyalty among his civil servants. This he achieved by courtesy and by method. He would never raise his voice, or 'bawl out' any of his staff, even on occasions when he might have been excused for doing so. Moreover, his practice of holding long, open discussions in his room was appreciated by senior and junior advisors alike. He sought the views of everyone, a flattering, if time-consuming, process, and it was generally considered to be time well spent. At the end of such sessions Heseltine would have developed a clear idea of the issues, and of the action required.

Heseltine's style was in marked contrast to that of his predecessors, and of those who have succeeded him. Traditionally, the secretary of state would call for formal submissions on reams of paper which he would then undertake to study, a process which often took a very long time.

What his civil servants particularly liked about Michael was his ability to generate ideas. Peter Shore, Peter Walker and others had tended to expect their advisors to come up with ideas from which, after due consideration, they would take their pick. It was refreshing to have a secretary of state who sparked ideas himself and in others, a process which encouraged an esprit de corps. He never hesitated to say if he thought mistakes had been made, but he took care not to single out individuals for blame. This again was something to which his civil servants had been unaccustomed. But if Heseltine himself had been involved in error, he would cheerfully accept responsibility for it.

Heseltine was sometimes severely tried. On one occasion his diary secretary sent him to 10 Downing Street for an important cabinet committee meeting only for Michael to find that the venue was elsewhere. He arrived eventually twenty minutes late. Even in such circumstances he was generally forbearing.

The view of him within his private office, and in the

department at large, was of a very private man who lacked a wide circle of close friends, but who was, even so, easy to relate to on both formal and informal occasions. He was looked on as being exceptionally generous towards those who worked closely with him, often taking his private secretaries out to dinner. What civil servants want most of their minister is clout; clout, that is, among his colleagues in general, and within the cabinet in particular. In the early 'eighties Michael was not to be found within the innermost cabinet circle, but he had the next best quality in the eyes of bureaucrats – competence. He expected his advisors to give him first class service but he never took such service for granted. He was always grateful when people made an extra effort. A former permanent secretary describes him as 'punctilious in his appreciation of what people did for him'. His annual Christmas parties were lavish events, involving hundreds of members of staff from the department. But Michael never dressed up as Santa Claus. Socially, he was good company. He enjoyed talking on a variety of topics, but did not monopolise the conversation any more than he did on duty. Michael listened at least as much as he talked. And he worked hard, arriving every morning at 8.30 rather than 9.15, and seldom leaving either for the House or home before 7.30 p.m. The department of the environment, which had not welcomed his appointment, was soon to be very pleasantly surprised.

What was the nature of Heseltine's inheritance? He had been put in charge of an enormously large government department involving the financing of 413 local authorities, through the rate support grant of taxpayers' money, a sum which amounted to one quarter of all public expenditure. The Property Services Agency (PSA), which is responsible for the whole of the government estate in land and assets, came under his umbrella. He was the protector of ancient buildings, and the defender of what was to become known as 'the environment'. Consciousness was growing of the extent to which industrial society had fouled its nest, and the political implications of this were soon to make themselves felt. The secretary of state, by using his statutory powers to override local planning decisions, could change the face of England in favour of the speculative builder or the conservationist. Landscape gardening is one of Heseltine's private passions; Mrs Thatcher had given him the country to play with.

His most important task, however, was to cut spending, and to reduce the number of his civil servants. The desire to reduce government spending was central to the Thatcher government's policy; local government spending was a principal target.

There was a plum in the pudding. The Conservatives were in favour of the sale of council houses to sitting tenants. This process, the gentrification of the council estates, had reinforced the Tory appeal to the more prosperous of the working class. It can be put in a somewhat wider context. Mrs Thatcher's great achievement has been to take power from the landed gents in the Tory Party and bestow it on the working classes. Working-class values are naturally conservative, linked to the idea of class, suspicious of change, wary of foreigners, armed with a cliché for every crisis. In the twenty years since Oxford the gents – once the upholders of right-wing values – have become moderate, and the 'players' right-wing. It is ironic that Michael Heseltine should have been, by the sale of council houses, an agent in a transformation he cannot have wished. Nevertheless, within a fortnight of his elevation he told parliament of his intention to sell the stock, and at a discount of between 30 and 50%.

The detail was left to John Stanley who was put in charge of the right-to-buy legislation. Heseltine set out to discover how his ministry actually worked. His predecessors had taken care to leave the day-to-day running of affairs to their permanent secretaries. If he were to 'manage' his department, Heseltine needed to discover the extent of its spending in order to determine where savings could be made. He examined each of the department's functions in turn.

This first glance at how everything worked swiftly developed into MINIS, the management information system Heseltine launched at the department of the environment in 1980. MINIS, like the William Orpen portrait of Lloyd George which, having been unearthed in Marsham Street, hung on the wall behind Michael's desk, travelled with him to the ministry of defence three years later. Heseltine believed that the 'managerial ethos' should apply as much to government as to the private sector. 'By managerial ethos,' he has said, 'I mean the process of examining what we are doing, setting realistic targets, fitting them to the resources available, and monitoring performance; and then, very important, telling people what the results are so that we can go back to the beginning of the loop and improve from there.'

The way MINIS functioned was disconcertingly simple. At environment where the hierarchy descends from the permanent secretary, to principal, to assistant secretary, to under-secretary and then to director, there are sixty-five heads. Each was required to define his tasks, the reason for doing them in the first place, and how much they cost. Some would have welcomed the intrusion; more would have thought the scheme an unnecessary impertinence. All suffered from a form of culture shock.

Thus Heseltine added a display of charts to his trappings of office. The advantage of MINIS was said to be that it was more systematic in its review of objectives, more precise in its definition of tasks and clearer in its presentation of results. And its supporters claimed it to have been responsible for large-scale sav.ngs. The more sceptical wondered whether it would 'travel'. In the event it did, to the ministry of defence, where a permanent secretary has described it as 'a nonsense'. A presentation by Michael of MINIS to the rest of the cabinet in early 1982 met with a less than enthusiastic response. Andrew Likierman, a lecturer at the London Business School, has concluded that 'the chances of widespread adoption must be slight, bearing in mind the strength of the opposition or merely indifference. Only if there is a major central initiative is the system likely to be adopted on a much more widespread basis.' Michael Heseltine is proud of his management skills and MINIS was one way of demonstrating them. Why should he be denied his vanity?

Heseltine's first major appointment was that of David Edmonds as his principal private secretary. He was one of four candidates for the post and was interviewed four times. Edmonds knew the department and its people, displayed an open mind and was as vigorous as he was articulate. From the start Edmonds devoted himself to the preparation of Michael Heseltine's major speeches in the House of Commons. (For his conference 'blockbuster', he could look only towards the research department at Central Office for help, as civil servants play no part in party, as opposed to government, matters.) Edmonds would reduce reams of turgid facts and figures to the bare essentials which would then be presented to Michael in palatable form. Heseltine would refine the draft still further, cutting out much of what detail remained; details which he might find hard to read, and his audience difficult to digest. The introduction and the peroration would be written by Heseltine himself. His sense of anticipation and his political feel meant that the secretary of state was seldom wrong-footed by events. He was described by one mandarin as 'laid-back' when under pressure, but then, as his business partners had often remarked, Heseltine had nerves of steel.

I spoke to Michael in October 1979 en route for the party conference at Blackpool. I asked him about Margaret. 'She flies,' he said, 'by the seat of her pants'; an uncharacteristic piece of familiarity. But he did admit that she could be deflected, 'and not only by Peter Carrington'. The conference that year was a triumphal progress, the party basking in the heat of its election victory, and Margaret Thatcher the Queen of the May. Michael's speech was rewarded, as ever, with a standing ovation. And he stuck, for once, more or less to his brief. My motive for reproducing some of it is to give the reader the flavour of the times.

Michael took as his theme 'Homes and Land'. Labour's

economic policies, he declared, 'coupled with its ill-judged dogma and administrative inertia' had put house building into severe decline. To correct this, the Tories had 'killed off the Community Land Act' and brought down Development Land Tax in the budget. The planning machinery, claimed Heseltine, was being subjected to a rigorous new discipline to convert those dusty files into decisions and results. (Decisions and results which were soon to alarm many ex-urban Conservatives.) And, claimed Heseltine finally, we have announced measures to get those vast sites which so disfigure our inner cities and are presently so often owned by local authorities and nationalised industries put up for sale and developed.

Heseltine knew all too well that his audience of the party faithful had a taste for denunciation. Abandoning the future in favour of the immediate past, he turned his guns upon the enemy. 'You would think,' he cried, flicking his hair out of his eyes, 'listening to some of the debates at Brighton' (where Labour had just held its conference) 'that the Labour government had never cut public expenditure.' The reality was somewhat different. 'When Labour was in power it was led by cabinet ministers who were, for five years, forced by their own incompetence to troop through the division lobby voting for public-expenditure cut after public-expenditure cut.' They would find any excuse, any distortion, however desperate, to avoid this 'one stark truth of Labour's rule. It was born in the tensions of the winter of 1973; it was haunted by misjudgement and prejudice and died in the very flames of discontent in 1979, which it had done so much to kindle five years before.'

This was rhetoric at its most effective, of a sort to which Tories were unaccustomed. Michael Foot could do the same thing for the Labour Party, but Conservatives spoke in less impassioned tones. Heseltine, lengthening his stride, continued: '. . .When the political barons of Labour's inner cities talk of "our people" it is not with trembling voice or dampening eye. It is "our people" in the sense of people owned and controlled and directed and employed. It is "our people", submissive, obedient, and, in the end, mobilised in the block votes of their feudal power. They slammed up the drawbridges of Manchester, Sheffield and London's East End not to defend their people, but to freeze them into a way of life and a standard of life, which, given the choice, these people would escape from at the earliest opportunity.' He mentioned (dropping his voice) that he had been asked whether extremist Labour authorities would be able to delay the purchase of council houses once the legislation was on the statute book. 'Not for a year, not for a month, not for a week, not for a day.'

It was heady stuff. And, for the time and place, right on the button. Over the sale of council houses the Conservative Party had stumbled on a winner, and Labour, sifting through the 1983 general election results, quietly abandoned their opposition to it. The Tory faithful, with nothing to look forward to save lunch, and Blackpool does not feature in the *Good Food Guide*, made a feast of the occasion. It was the 'glad, confident morning' of the Thatcher era.

New brooms do not always sweep as clean as they would wish. The Housing Bill, which would oblige local authorities to sell council houses, ran up hard against the parliamentary timetable. MPs do not like sitting into August, when beaches beckon, to say nothing of the grouse. On 5 August it became clear that the bill would not be through in time to receive the royal assent. This was due to obstructive tactics on the part of some Labour MPs who objected strongly to the government's refusal to accept an amendment passed in the Lords which would exempt sheltered accommodation and housing for the elderly. After much huffing, Heseltine, Stanley and the government whips were forced to accept the amendment, which they did on 7 August.

On the following Sunday the *Observer* carried an adversely critical article of Heseltine entitled 'A Tarnished Term for the Golden Boy'. Tarnished or not, the use of the term 'Golden Boy', without acknowledgement to Clifford Odets, gives a taste of how Heseltine had come to be regarded even by one of the 'heavier' Sundays. Was he really the coming man, or simply too good to be true? Eight years later we have still to find the answer.

The *Observer* quoted the opinions of two Labour MPs. 'In one respect he is very like Margaret Thatcher. They both like to make bold declarations of policy to please the party zealots. Then they run up against the practical snags. He is inflexible. When all the evidence suggests he'd better settle for 80%, he will lose his pants trying to get 100%. In my view the arrogance of the man will be his undoing.' Another said, 'The trouble with Michael is that he doesn't always have a complete grasp of the subjects he is dealing with. I just don't think he works hard enough. What he employs is the grandeur and rhetoric of politics, but he doesn't know the details. He is a very much nicer man than some of the others in the present cabinet. He is liberal on social issues, against capital punishment; anti-racist. He is by no means an Identi-kit Conservative.' The anonymous critic, who sounds like a former Labour minister, continued, 'One of his problems is that because of the general view of him as rather lightweight, he doesn't carry weight in the Commons.'

'Nice chap', 'arrogant', 'lightweight' and lazy; so many contradictions reveal the uncertainty with which he was regarded, and not just by Labour MPs. Whatever else he may have been he was not idle. He was more than a 'first-class front-of-house manager'. He had managed in three months to galvanise a fearful ministry, to speed up decisions on structure plans (blueprints for the development of a county or city) and to get a controversial bill onto the statute book.

A cabinet minister in charge of a great department of state is not only the spokesman for, and indeed, the defender of, his ministry within the cabinet itself, he has an obligation to implement policies agreed by it. The Thatcher cabinet held strong views as to what should be done. It had two priorities with regard to the department of the environment. The government wished to make certain that local government spending was contained within the overall targets and, as we have seen, local government spending amounted to a quarter of all public expenditure; and secondly, to hold down increases in local rates as part of the counter-inflation policy. These aims could be guaranteed to bring Heseltine into conflict with the local authorities, both Labour, which controlled many of the cities, and Conservative, which ruled the shires. Traditionally, the Tories had made much of the 'independence' of local government; the doctrine that 'the man in Whitehall knows best' was attributed to the Labour Party. However, the twin aims of Mrs Thatcher's first administration were nothing if not interventionist. Thatcher and Heseltine clearly knew best what was good for local government.

The arguments needed to sustain so revolutionary a doctrine acquired a gloss of their own. It was asserted by ministers that the 'old implicit consensus' about relations between national and local government had broken down. According to this view, up to the mid-1970s local authorities of all parties had broadly accepted the right of central government to set limits on spending. Hence, when local councils were considering spending above the desired level, Westminster, if not Whitehall, had a duty to intervene. The more so as the taxpayer financed on average three-fifths of current spending through the rate support grant.

The block grant was to be the new weapon of intervention. This device was designed not simply to influence the total spent by local authorities but to control the particular. The block grant worked in this way: up till then, grants had been allocated on the basis of past spending, so that the authorities which spent more automatically received more. The new system was intended to relate the grant more closely to standard spending levels by what are known as 'grant related expenditures'. These are stated benchmarks based on the principles of equalising differences in local rateable values and of assessing spending needs. This did not stop councils from deciding their own levels of expenditure or of rates, but the block grant discouraged overspending, in that when a council's spending rose above the benchmark level, the government progressively reduced the rate of grant, which forced Labour councils to raise rates in order to cover their additional spending.

In addition, the government set separate targets for reductions in expenditure which differed from the stated benchmarks, so some councils faced conflicting targets. Not surprisingly, this system provoked confusion and criticism, not least among Conservatives in local government who loyally introduced policies of restraint only to receive ever-diminishing amounts of money from the block grant. Virtue, apparently, was no longer its own reward.

It was not long before the screw was given another turn. Many Labour local authorities which, to do them justice, controlled areas of relative deprivation, continued to increase their spending well above the Whitehall targets, and, in consequence, to levy big rate rises; Lambeth was one example. In consequence, Heseltine was obliged to bring in further legislation to abolish supplementary rates and to allow the department of the environment to adjust the block grant paid to individual authorities to encourage reductions in spending. Heseltine also introduced a series of other measures to restrict local authorities, such as tighter regulations concerning the operation of direct labour and more extensive auditing of local authorities.

Thus, for the whole of his three and a half years as secretary of state for the environment, Heseltine was in the thick of it. The results of his policies were pretty unsatisfactory, both for many local authorities and many ratepayers. The leftwards drift within the Labour Party threw up a series of left-wing Labour councillors and councils and the Labour Party, frustrated in the Commons by the government's majority, took the 'war' on to the streets. Ratepayers became increasingly angry, and demands for fundamental reform of the rating system, first trailed by Mrs Thatcher as long ago as the general election of October 1974, grew in intensity. A green paper, prepared by a ministerial committee with the help of the department of the environment, showed how difficult the alternatives to rates were, and indeed still are. A complicated package of modest reforms was rejected by the Prime Minister and the cabinet in January 1983.

Heseltine's policies towards local government spending pleased no one. Critics, and not just of the Left, argued that there had been no real problem of local overspending and that tight targets and cuts in the rate support grant had simply had the effect of transferring more of the burden on to the ratepayer. Professors Jones and Stewart (1983) argued that local government spending had fallen since the mid-'seventies as a proportion of total public spending, but this was mainly owing to a very large fall in capital investment, especially new house building. Local authority current expenditure had continued to rise both absolutely and relative to total public spending, from 21.8% in '78/'79 to 22.7% in '82/'83. And this rise was despite a 4.8% reduction in staff numbers in the first two years of the Thatcher government.

The cabinet was aiming for a much lower level of spending, and failed to get it. This failure reflected, in part, the battle between 'wets' and 'dries', in which the more moderate members of Mrs Thatcher's first cabinet fought a rearguard action to protect their budgets. Alone among the 'big spenders', Patrick Jenkin, who was at that time at the department of health and social security, volunteered to make greater sacrifices.

In short, local authority current spending was up, its capital spending down. As a result many ratepayers faced substantially higher rate increases in parts of London and elsewhere than even the doubling of the rate level which was the fate of most ratepayers. At the beginning of 1983 it could be said that Heseltine's series of expedients to deal with local authority expenditure had failed either to control spending or to produce an acceptable constitutional balance between Whitehall and the rights of local authorities and ratepayers. The government had intervened but the ratepayers felt oppressed. In the Tory manifesto for the June 1983 election, the party undertook to abolish the Greater London Council and the metropolitan councils, a task which destroyed the reputation of Heseltine's successor at the department of the environment, the pedestrian Patrick Jenkin. Whether Michael could have dealt with Ken Livingstone as successfully as he did with Bruce Kent and Joan Ruddock, we shall never know. Clearly, Jenkin did not.

As secretary of state for the environment, Michael Heseltine set out to do Mrs Thatcher's bidding. Heseltine's belief that the private sector had been shamefully neglected under Labour meant that the balance between public and private had to be redressed. And the 'victory' over inflation, to the achievement of which the government had given priority, compelled reductions of public expenditure. The unexpected severity of the recession took the Thatcher government by surprise, but the Prime Minister was happy to take what advantage she could from it. If local government spending was a prime target for economy, retrenchment fell most heavily on the housing programme for which Heseltine was responsible.

The Environment Select Committee of the Commons noted in a report published in 1980 that 'the present government's strategy of reducing public expenditure thus relies principally on the achievement of the planned reduction in housing expenditure'. Unlike those in most other programmes, this reduction occurred. New public sector house completions fell from 104,000 in 1979 (itself down from 160,000 in the mid-'seventies) to 49,200 in 1982, the lowest level since the 1920s. Over the same period council rents more than doubled in cash terms as subsidies from central government and from rate funds were cut by more than 50% in real terms. That was the measure of Heseltine's success (or failure).

It is impossible to judge Heseltine without trying to understand what it was that he was doing. The government's aim was to introduce and extend market forces, both by requiring the local authority sector to be self-financing and profit-making and by reducing the size of the public sector. Heseltine tilted the balance between public and private by pushing up council rents while maintaining the tax relief subsidies on mortgage interest. This, when taken with the sale of council houses to sitting tenants, added up to a giant step in the direction of that Conservative goal of 'a property owning democracy' about which Anthony Eden in particular had spoken.

Whether one supports this notion or not, the results of Heseltine's policies were dramatic. About half a million council houses and flats were sold between the two general elections, when altogether there was an increase of one million owner-occupiers. As a result, the percentage of owner-occupied households rose from just under 54% to nearly 59% over the period in England and Wales, the largest change since 1945. A rash of custom-built front doors appeared over the council estates of England; something that was not without its political rewards. According to one study, purchasers of council houses were strongly pro-Conservative. Of those who had bought their houses, 56% voted Tory and only 18% Labour. Of those who had voted Labour in '79, and had then bought their council houses, 59% switched to the Conservatives or to the Alliance. Moreover, Labour did badly in the new towns. The 'Falklands factor' was not the sole explanation for the Tory win in June 1983.

Heseltine's wish to increase council house rents had led to the Battle of the Black Rod, a parliamentary fracas of an unprecedented nature which took place on 13 November 1979 at the fag end of the session. Heseltine had announced, by the publication of an answer to a written question, a consultative document which outlined increases in rents of £2.50 to £3 a week. Ministers of all sorts have published information in this way, and some still do, at the eleventh hour, thereby avoiding a statement to the House and subsequent debate. A similar exercise was mounted in July 1986, when the adversely critical report of the Select Committee of

Defence on Westland was published. The result predictably is uproar.

Whether parliamentary rage is synthetic or genuine is neither here nor there. On 13 November the Labour benches, their morale sapped by defeat and by the imposition of policies to which they strongly objected, exploded. Labour MPs physically prevented the arrival of Black Rod, an official of the palace whose task is to summon the Commons to begin the ceremonies which should mark the end of the session. Michael Heseltine was summoned by the government whips from his office in the Commons to defend his action. Such was the disorder that Speaker Thomas suspended the House to allow tempers to cool.

When the House resumed, Heseltine had disappeared. Mrs Thatcher was seen to be anything but amused. Just as the speaker was about to announce the second suspension, Heseltine arrived hotfoot from the library to explain that he had been seeking for precedents and, what was more, had found them. At this the government benches became bored (Labour MPs were still on their feet), and after a word from the chief whip Heseltine announced the withdrawal of the offending document. It wasn't much of a victory for the Opposition, for the document was promptly reintroduced later that month; but for Michael Heseltine, the affair resembled that of the mace, but in reverse.

The house had been in a quite extraordinary state of turmoil. Mr Nicholas Fairbairn, the solicitor general for Scotland, a man for whom the popular press reserves the adjective 'colourful', said angrily, 'This was mob rule. Robespierre had his place, but I was prevented from leaving the Chamber. They assaulted me; they punched me. It was dreadful.' Old scores had clearly been paid off. Not to be outdone, Clive Soley, Labour MP for Hammersmith North, protested, 'There was pushing, kicking and shoving. I had my foot trampled on . . . this was the Tory Party behaving like the louts it is so quick to condemn at football matches.'

Humbug is the essential lubricant of public life. Neverthe-less, Heseltine had, by taking a short cut, lit a fuse of frustration on the Labour benches, where he was not loved at the best of times. Widely, if unfairly, regarded as a rich property speculator, he was also feared for his political skills, not least his anti-socialist rhetoric. He also appeared to be the cutting edge of 'Thatcherism', a term of abuse which was coming into fashion. Tall, well-suited, wearing kipper ties and flamboyant shirts, Heseltine seemed to take pleasure in his task of cutting the number of council houses, selling off the best of the stock and now putting up the rents. Michael, it appeared, was wholeheartedly playing the role of Mr Hyde; it was to be some time before Dr Jekyll came to the fore.

In the Commons, Heseltine was 'shadowed' at environ-ment by Gerald Kaufman. This was clever matchmaking by Michael Foot who chose the most acerbic of Labour's front-bench performers. Kaufman, Heseltine's Oxford con-temporary and Union rival, set out to cut him down to size. Described by Andrew Roth in his Commons handbook as 'smilingly sinister', Kaufman masks the fact that he is on the right of the Labour Party with his tongue. Were he a dressing he would consist of five parts vinegar to one of oil.

According to Kaufman, a Heseltine statement to the House was 'one of the most disgraceful and contemptible ever made ... contemptible in its dishonesty and disgraceful in its content'. The secretary of state was both fraudulent and cynical. Michael's response was typical of his customary coolness in the face of obvious provocation. Of the rival strands within his personality – caution on one hand, over-reaction on the other – calculation won the day. His response to Kaufman's opening barrage, mounted to celebrate his new front-bench appointment, was tactfully bland. 'I hope the House will not misunderstand me if, first, I welcome the Rt Hon. Gentleman. We have been friends since Oxford days [not true]. I hope very much that the friendship will survive the onslaught the House has just heard. I should like, in that spirit, to help him with some of the figures.' They were indeed well matched, and Kaufman got his reward. He was elected top of the poll in the shadow cabinet elections in 1982.

As secretary of state for the environment, Heseltine anticipated the 'Greens', a movement which was to grow steadily in importance throughout his term of office, but which reached its peak under his successor, Patrick Jenkin. The so-called Green Movement in defence of the nation's backyard, began as a left-wing protest against what many saw as the fouling of the nest. It reinforced more conventional bodies such as the Campaign for the Preservation of Rural England. Its concerns included the protection of listed buildings, the rate of housing development both within and beyond the green belts, anxiety about the environmental effects of motorway building, and a generalised hostility towards nuclear power. As with all causes that attract the right-minded, for who would not want to protect the Wenlock Edge from quarrying or prevent the erection of skyscrapers in Greenwich, it slides into extravagance. By the time the Tory shires had mobilised to protect their countryside from housing development, Heseltine had been moved to the ministry of defence. Jenkin failed to mollify the counties, just as he failed to defuse Ken Livingstone; it was left to his successor, Kenneth Baker, to adapt skilfully to the new pressures. However, if Heseltine had courted unpopularity by his policy of cutting local government spending and putting up council house rents, on environmental matters he could claim to be on the side of the angels.

In 1979 he had intervened to prevent Francis Pym, the secretary of state for defence, who was of course a cabinet colleague, from demolishing his stately home, Hazells Hall in Bedfordshire. Pym, who had built a new house nearby, had found the old one surplus to his requirements. Flushed with success, Heseltine then refused British Rail permission to alter the Victorian booking hall at St Pancras station, and agreed to the establishment of a green belt around Cambridge. Later he destroyed the 'Green Goddess', a monstrous skyscraper scheduled for erection on the south bank of the Thames near Lambeth Bridge. He even unveiled a statue by Henry Moore in Kensington Gardens. Michael was clearly no philistine.

In September 1980 Heseltine was embarrassed by newspaper reports that he was to be taken to court by Swansea Council. A cottage owned by his mother had been allowed to fall into disrepair. Such a hiccup should not be permitted to spoil his record. He may well have gazed down upon London from the seventeenth floor of his Marsham Street office and mused as to how best to stamp his mark on the metropolis. He was no Nash or Wren, but he was responsible for decisions the consequences of which Londoners will be obliged to live with for some time.

In the week before Christmas 1982, in what Heseltine himself announced as 'a momentous week in the history of the architecture of London', he gave details of four plans. They were: a million square feet of offices on the South Bank next to the National Theatre; the conversion of the old Billingsgate fishmarket into a commodity exchange, with a large blue office block attached; a major new development on the site of St George's Hospital, Hyde Park Corner; and the appointment as architects of the National Gallery's new extension in Trafalgar Square of a London firm whose designs for the building had been vehemently rejected by the gallery's trustees. This was the design that the Prince of Wales was to describe as 'a monstrous carbuncle'.

Heseltine's enthusiasm for his role as the Queen's Architect was evidenced by his speech to the Royal Institute of British Architects. 'Future generations will judge the quality of our contribution by the quality of the architecture we leave behind.' He went on to warn of short-term expediency. 'Long after the day-to-day political battles are forgotten, the buildings will remain.' He can be forgiven the truism. Besides the rejuvenation of London's docklands, he can claim responsibility for the Government Conference Centre built opposite Westminster Abbey in what was one of the last surviving bomb sites in Britain. The huge Vauxhall Cross redevelopment close to the Tate, and the refurbishment of the old Langham Hotel, will become monuments to Heseltine's time in office. Perhaps he should best be remembered for what he saved from the demolition men: Giles Gilbert Scott's cathedral-like Battersea Power Station.

Michael Heseltine has two major political successes to his credit: the defeat of the Campaign for Nuclear Disarmament in 1983 and his brief period as Viceroy of Liverpool, 'minister for Merseyside' in 1981–2. The Westland affair was a personal defeat of a magnitude which may yet deny him his objective, the leadership of the Conservative Party and the premiership. It was a bigger defeat for Leon Brittan, the minister who opposed him, and a severe setback for the Prime Minister to whom the Tory Party gave the benefit of the doubt. She had willed the ends; she should have taken responsibility for the means. But for that story I must ask the reader to be patient.

The events of 1981 had much to do with the primacy of Mrs Thatcher herself. She is a woman about whom it is hard to be neutral. Her character seems to many to combine insecurity with self-confidence, an unhappy blend which does not appeal to all her colleagues. I have described her as 'tart, obstinate and didactic' and she possesses all those traits. She has also a capacity to inspire loyalty and affection among those who feel and think about politics as she does. Despite their mutual dislike, Heath and Thatcher have things in common: a humble background, an impatience with opposition, and a capacity for hard work. Politically they are poles apart, each standing at the opposite ends of the Conservative spectrum. Heath has been unlucky; Margaret has enjoyed more than her share of good fortune. Had Sir Alec Douglas-Home stayed on to fight the doomed election of 1966 (thus saving Heath from the opprobrium of defeat) and had Edward Heath gone to the country a week earlier than he did in February 1974, the course of history might well have been different. And by the same token, had not General Galtieri embarked on the invasion of the Falklands in April 1982, Mrs Thatcher might not have survived to enjoy a second term. But who can tell? The charm of politics lies in its unpredictability. What can be asserted is that by the spring of 1981 she was in trouble. What part, if any, did Michael Heseltine play in the affair?

The answer can only be 'precious little'. In the year-long battle between 'wets' and 'dries', between the traditional Tories and the party's 'arditi' (the ardent ones), Michael took care not to take sides. Although an interventionist and no friend of Margaret's, he told David Lipsey in an article in *New Society* five years later 'I was never a "wet" in the soft sense.' Yet the 'wets' – an unpleasant nickname, invented by Mrs Thatcher herself and adopted by those so identified as a badge of distinction analogous to the 'desert rats', expected Michael to rally to their side. In the arguments in the cabinet in 1981 over future public spending, Heseltine certainly urged generosity, but he refused to join any cabal against the Prime Minister. Such circumspection did not make him friends among Mrs Thatcher's allies, who still, taking their cue from 'Herself', regarded him as being 'not one of us'. By the same token, the 'wets' talked of betrayal, and of Heseltine's facility 'not to be able to see a parapet without ducking below it'. Over Westland he was to build his own parapet and dance naked upon it.

The depth of the recession, rising unemployment and riots on the streets of Brixton in London and Toxteth in Liverpool, deepened cabinet discontents. The April budget with its swingeing increases in taxes almost drove Prior, Gilmour and Walker to resign. St John Stevas, Carlisle and Soames were sacked, so too was Sir Ian Gilmour. In their stead were recruited true believers such as Tebbit, Lawson, Parkinson and Biffen. Mrs Thatcher's speechwriters came up with phrases like 'the Lady's not for turning', and Mrs Thatcher, exercising the levers of power, pulled through. The treasury had to give way a little, an additional five billions of public spending was authorised, but much of that was the consequence of the recession itself. Only when Mrs Thatcher crossed swords publicly with Whitelaw on the issue of law and order at the 1981 party conference at Blackpool did she appear to be in real danger. But moderation was not the ideal rallying cry, and the backbenchers, most of whom were on the right of the party, stayed loyal to her brand of conviction politics. Heseltine, by thowing his weight against the treasury, probably felt he had done his bit. It was the street riots of 1981 which were to offer him his biggest test to date.

The inexorable rise in crime has continued to be a matter of acute political embarrassment for Mrs Thatcher. In 1979 and in 1983 she presented herself as the leader of the party of law and order. We have now reached a plateau of impotence on which Norman Tebbit preaches against the so-called 'Permissive Society', while the home secretary extracts what money he can from the treasury for police and prisons. That the inner-city riots of 1981, which were to afford Heseltine his opportunity to do something about conditions in Liverpool in particular, were linked with crime was clearly established by Lord Scarman in his famous report.

Scarman wrote: 'Any attempt to resolve the circumstances from which the disorders of this year spring cannot therefore be limited to recommendations about policing but must embrace the wider social context in which policing is carried out.' And within the limits of his terms of reference Lord Scarman stressed the failure of many attempts to tackle the problems of inner-city decline. Scarman called for a better coordinated attack both on these general economic and social difficulties, and, specifically, on racial disadvantage. He noted that this might mean that 'ethnic minorities will enjoy for a time positive discrimination in their favour'. To this last suggestion the government has turned a deaf ear, fearful of the wrath of many of its supporters, not least the 'emancipated', that is, council-house-owning members of the Conservative working class. The success of action taken within the United States to improve the lot of blacks has been ignored.

While the more enlightened Tories such as the home secretary, William Whitelaw, looked with favour upon the thrust of Lord Scarman's report, its conclusions gave little comfort to Mrs Thatcher and to those Conservatives who feel as she does. She found it difficult to accept the implied relationship between unemployment, social deprivation and crime; to many party activists crime is crime regardless of any mitigating circumstances. Even Norman Tebbit, whose contribution to finding a solution to rising crime was the discovery of sin, was chary of admitting that the devil finds work for idle hands. Yet the prospect of the derelict centres of once prosperous British cities being put to the torch for reasons of frustration, despair or just devilment, served to concentrate wonderfully the mind of Her Majesty's government. After Toxteth burnt, Michael Heseltine was told to set up a Merseyside task force, composed of representatives from government departments and people seconded from the private sector, whose job it was to work with local authorities and interests in the area. Michael Heseltine had always been an interventionist in an administration which claimed to believe in laissez faire; he was now to intervene, and to do so with a vengeance.

On 5 July 1981 Toxteth, a run-down district of central Liverpool where once elegant Georgian terraced houses had succumbed to multioccupancy, and tower blocks stood isolated in a wasteland of dereliction, was set alight by rioters, mainly black youths. Toxteth, coming as it did after Brixton, caused the sound of the tumbril to be heard as far south as Conservative strongholds such as Hartley Wintney. On 6 July it was announced that Michael Heseltine would visit Toxteth. Mr Hyde was to change to Dr Jekyll.

The Toxteth riot postponed press speculation about an issue which had surfaced in *The Times* diary in June – that Heseltine might replace Lord Thorneycroft as party chairman. In the event, the job went to Cecil Parkinson whose presentational skills were almost as well developed as Heseltine's, but whose relationship with Mrs Thatcher was much more intimate. The 'Heseltine for Smith Square' movement has been, among Tories, a recurring fever, for his talent for communication would seem to be marvellously well-suited for the task. Whether he would have subjected that bureaucratic machine to the rigours of MINIS, we shall never know, but his photogeneity and gift of the gab could have served the party well. His name was put forward again when a successor was sought for John Selwyn Gummer, but Tebbit's views were more in harmony with the Prime Minister's.

The fires of Toxteth distracted public attention from the row over Heseltine's decision not to allow the coal board to engage in opencast coal mining in the Vale of Belvoir. The miners and the Labour Party were, predictably enough, annoyed, but every other interest in the East Midlands breathed again. The Opposition moved a motion of censure against him in the Commons, but the challenge was easily deflected.

Michael Heseltine did not arrive in Liverpool until 20 July. On 17th *The Times* carried an interview with him in which he indicated that he saw 'urban regeneration' as his most urgent commitment. 'It is everything I want to see happening, and I will devote every resource to it that I possibly can.' However, the article went on to point out that Heseltine had reduced grant support away from the cities to what were seen as the less needy shires. He had also threatened to penalise the so-called overspending local authorities, many of which were Labour-controlled and in the inner cities.

This apparent contradiction could best be explained by Heseltine's long-standing distrust of non-productive sub-sidies. He wanted to see instead more capital investment in buildings, infrastructure and schemes for generalised environmental improvement. There should be, argues Hesel-tine, a partnership between the public and private sectors in order to bring about improvement. Doubters were entitled to point out that it was capital spending which had so far borne the brunt of the Thatcher government's public-spending cuts, and that the department of the environment's housing programme had suffered more than any other. To this charge, Heseltine could offer one of two answers: either that capital cuts were easier to achieve and quicker in effect, for reducing revenue expenditure took time; or that 'victory' over inflation remained the government's overriding economic objective.

Heseltine arrived in Liverpool trailing a retinue composed of the corps d'élite of the nation's press. They followed Michael's progress around the city in a chartered bus, buttonholing the bewildered and the aggrieved, leaving no stone unturned. In their spare time the press sought out the Cavern, the nightclub in a cellar where the Beatles had sparked the renaissance of the 'sixties, and, having filed their copy ('Tarzan in the Corrugated Jungle'), recruited themselves in one of the Chinese restaurants for which the city is famed. The parliamentary session may have been drawing to a bad-tempered close, but Heseltine's descent upon Liverpool was the best of copy.

On 21 July John Young, the planning reporter of *The Times*, told his readers that 'Heseltine tells Merseyside he brings no pot of gold'. Heseltine, standing in front of a phalanx of floodlights, TV cameras and microphones, told the world that his task was not to perform a Lord Scarman exercise on Toxteth. But, in view of the traumas that had shaken the nation in the past few weeks, any government would have to listen to people and discuss the reasons for such events. Heseltine repeatedly emphasised that he had come to Liverpool to listen and not to give advice. 'The idea that we can get a dramatic solution in two weeks just does not make any sense.'

In the past he had been criticised for telling local people what to do but never staying long enough to listen. 'I am now putting that right. There is anxiety that a large number of people who administer policies do not live in the areas affected and do not have close contact with the problems.'

The long-term objectives should be the maintenance of confidence, the creation of new opportunities, and bringing together of communities which had perhaps drifted too far apart, the removal of the sense of hopelessness and 'an attempt to challenge the assumption that nobody, takes seriously what people here are thinking and saying'. It was at this juncture that the secretary of state entered his caveat against unlimited spending.

He had not come to look specifically at the problems of Toxteth or Liverpool 8, but at the state of the whole city. Unemployment was, he thought, the central feature of the challenge. If people wanted to make points about the way the police carried out their duties and about their relationship with the community, he was ready to listen.

The idea of a three-week, highly publicised visit to Liverpool was Heseltine's own. He won Mrs Thatcher's approval (the proposal did not come before the full cabinet) for what was a brilliantly conceived political gesture, and one, what is more, that has had useful consequences. Heseltine was fortunate in that the spadework which he had done in 1979 on his appointment as secretary of state, the setting up of the Urban Development Corporation and with it the genesis of the Garden Festival which was later to enliven Liverpool, came to fruition in the months after the Toxteth riot.

The equivocation with which journalists regarded Heseltine can be illustrated by a quotation from a piece by Philip Norman in *The Sunday Times*: '. . . His appearance is still *Town* personified. The suit is grey but not ministerially so, its texture soft, its shade expensively vague. The coat sits perfectly in any posture. The trousers fall, negligently but exactly, over black shoes that do not require polishing. Both the shirt and the tie could well feature in their own quarter-page ads. As he walks he pushes back one or other of the wings of heavy blond hair which have carried him so high in his Leader's favour. Television lights emphasise his deep suntan and pure gold eyelashes.' Norman at least gives Heseltine credit for not doing as Quintin Hogg did in the 'sixties when he visited the 'depressed' North-East, namely wearing a cloth cap. Michael would not have been seen dead in a cloth cap.

Heseltine was clearly moved by the squalor he saw on his 'walk about' in Croxteth and Toxteth, and the press recognised this. Philip Norman wrote of the women of Croxteth who began by shouting 'Why don't you come and look at the shit we live in?' but ended by saying thank you and even bobbing a little. 'There was a moment', wrote Norman, 'when he emerged from a flat, flooded four weeks ago, deprived of light, heat and water since then, and last weekend smashed to pieces by teenage vandals. The minister's black town shoe crunched over the broken crockery and doll's furniture which the young householder had not nerved himself to touch. "What a shattering experience. I am sorry," Heseltine said. The young man watched him go with a sort of face you see on a deathbed pillow, murmured, "Goodbye, thanks very much." '

Later, when asked what he had felt on seeing the conditions under which the other half lived, he said, 'They're dreadful; dreadful.' He was asked what had impressed him most on his visit so far. 'The children. The impact on the children.' Not even a journalist could doubt that his sentiments were genuine. Poverty has always brought out the Lloyd George side of Michael Heseltine.

On 31 July a photograph of Heseltine trying unsuccessfully to knock a wall over in Bootle with a bulldozer was carried by most of the national newspapers, presumably for its symbolic effect.

On 4 August Michael inveigled a remarkable collection of top businessmen from all over Britain to visit Merseyside. Liverpool had, in recent years, been abandoned by the banks and the insurance companies, shipping had declined drastically in importance as trade with Europe, rather than with the Americas, had become the more important. Among indigenous businesses, Littlewoods, the pools, mail order and stores empire founded by Sir John Moores, who had begun life as a Liverpool postman, was the most prominent. But the city itself had become famous, not for its industry, and not even for its commerce, but for the Beatles and its two rival football clubs. Ethnically a mix of Irish, Chinese and West Indians, the Liverpudlians have a reputation for anarchic wit and a taste for leisure which the more old-fashioned Lancashire man would describe as 'work-shy'. But there was very little work about.

The businessmen were put into a bus with Heseltine, microphone in hand, acting as guide. They included Robin Leigh Pemberton, then Chairman of NatWest; a general manager of the Midland; Timothy Hugh Bevan, the Chairman of Barclays, and Sir Jeremy Morse, Chairman of Lloyds. This cluster of bankers was reinforced by chairmen and chief executives from the Abbey National, Woolwich and the Nationwide. In all, thirty or so leading financial and City figures spent a day on board a charabanc, touring the streets of Liverpool. That Heseltine should have persuaded so many to quit the Thames for the Mersey is a tribute to his powers of persuasion, and a testament to the shock which the country had been given by the riots of that summer.

Heseltine's aim was to demonstrate to them the fact that conditions in all Britain's major cities were worsening, and that the political consequences of dereliction would affect everyone. 'It is just not possible for the trustees of the nation's savings, based in the City of London, to ignore these problems,' Heseltine told them. It was a theme which he was to return to after his resignation in January 1986.

Heseltine also wished to persuade his guests to donate for a year one of their brightest young managers, whose salary they would continue to pay. They would work in conjunction with people from the public sector on schemes to revitalise the city. There were signs of interest, but few were in a position to commit themselves. In the event, the scheme never got off the ground.

Cast in the role of master of ceremonies, Heseltine described himself as the 'light relief' among so many experts.

The press, ensconced in the back of the bus but denied a crate of light ale, dutifully reported the odyssey. The bus first stopped at the largely derelict South Docks. John Young of *The Times* wrote: 'our convoy drove past gaunt and ghostly warehouses, weed-infested wharves surrounding dock basins choked with slime and mud.' Near the entrance to the Mersey Tunnel, which, when it was opened in the 'thirties, was one of the country's engineering marvels, they saw the shells of two tower blocks which the council had dynamited two years before, but could not afford to replace. They went on to visit the concrete towers of Everton, which, on close inspection, revealed a dismal picture of rusting corrugated iron, broken windows and graffiti. Garlanded with cameras, Heseltine led the way, the businessmen in tow. An urchin told them cheerfully that he, for one, enjoyed smashing things up.

It was some Progress. Wherever Heseltine went he was recognised, and children surrounded him as if he were urging them to join a crusade. In a city of footballers and pop singers, Heseltine was a star. Robin Leigh Pemberton, when asked by the press as to his intentions, said that he had already been to Liverpool 'more than once'. He agreed that NatWest might be persuaded to 'identify' its investment; but it had to be remembered that there were many other deserving cases.

On 6 August, the nation having been the witness of much toing and froing, and with the secretary of state rarely absent from the television screen, *The Times* attempted a summing-up. Magisterially, the leader writer opined that Heseltine went to Merseyside declaring that he had no pot of gold on offer, and had come out having offered none. Nonetheless (he wrote), the care and concern he had shown on his three-week excursion into the urban wilderness had earned him a great deal of respect, but it would have to be quickly converted into results if the city was not to become once more disillusioned with politicians' concern doing nothing to arrest its decline.

The writer, balancing one subordinate clause against the other, pointed out that the summary package offered to

Liverpool mostly consisted of items giving notice that local authorities and other agencies would make a special effort to do things that they were already willing enough to do. The funds were apparently to come from existing hard-pressed local allocations. He concluded, 'there is little here that has not been tried over and over again. Part of the tragedy of Toxteth and Brixton is that there is little disagreement about what needs to be done on the ground. The problem is how to make sure that it gets done.' In this pessimistic conclusion, *The Times* noted that action of any kind could at best only hope to stem the decline until a general revival of the economy brought new opportunity. Meanwhile it was especially important not to waste the funds that were available.

Had Heseltine been wasting his time? Philip Jordan wrote in the *Guardian* a piece entitled 'The Minister Came and Saw, can he Conquer?' to the effect that Heseltine had certainly made his presence felt on Merseyside. He had conducted what he himself had called 'the longest period of listening a minister has ever given a region'. He had begun (wrote Jordan) his visit with an empty diary and, realising that if he were to use his time productively he would have to take the initiative, rather than wait for Merseyside to come and see him, Heseltine soon launched into a series of meetings and tours which far exceeded the planned twelve-hour working day.

The days began with a pre-breakfast briefing. A crowded schedule followed, involving missed meals for many of his twenty-four-strong working group, and a series of working breakfasts, lunches and dinners for Heseltine. In a space of three weeks he met community leaders, local politicians, youth workers, sportsmen, industrialists, ship owners, housing experts and any number of council tenants. The official 'end of the day' was at 9.30 p.m. Often Heseltine and his team worked through into the small hours. It was, on Michael Hesletine's part, a vivid demonstration of his stamina and his will to work.

So overwhelming was the public response, British Telecom

engineers hastily had to lay on extra telephone lines as hundreds of calls jammed the Heseltine team's temporary switchboard. Many hundreds of letters arrived each day, Heseltine promising a reply to each one. One member of the team said afterwards, 'It's been as if every person in the city was saying, "Well, you've come to listen to our problems, here we are and this is what I think you should do about them." '

David Edmonds, Heseltine's private secretary, said, 'In twelve years in the civil service I've never worked so hard. My day has been from eight in the morning to one or two o'clock in the morning. I've been six years in the private office in London and there was nothing like this.' The only break Heseltine allowed himself to take was a trip to London for the wedding of Prince Charles and Lady Diana. However, he was back in Liverpool late that evening to attend a meeting of the Merseyside Community Relations Council. At the time I described him in a piece I wrote in the *Daily Telegraph* as being 'as strong as a horse'.

A liberal of the Hampstead school, Michael was genuinely shocked by the privation and the squalor he saw in Liverpool. Brought up in comfortable circumstances, he had had, save for a few months in the army, little contact with the working class. He never shared the petit bourgeois contempt and impatience for the poor which other prominent Conservatives strive to hide, if not from each other, then from the world at large. Never in a thousand years could Michael have 'done a Tebbit' and urged the unemployed to do as his father once did and 'get on their bikes'. He knew enough about the rigidities of public housing and their effect upon the mobility of labour ever to have been tempted to do so. And had he been as ignorant as Tebbit, he would have taken care to bite his tongue.

He managed to impress nearly everyone he met. He held an impromptu get-together with a gang of young blacks on the back of a van parked on a piece of wasteland. He impressed groups of local industrialists with his knowledge and concern, and even Labour MPs who met him for an hour and emerged with no promises seemed mesmerised. James Dunn, MP for Liverpool, Kirkdale, said publicly, 'I'd say it was the most encouraging meeting I've ever attended. He is in no doubt about the real problems on Merseyside.'

Although the treasury had prevented him from making Liverpool a present of 'a pot of gold', it was widely agreed that his energy and sense of commitment had had a very favourable impact upon the community. His presence in the city, which some were to dub 'viceregal', seemed to carry conviction. Despite Mrs Thatcher's free-market rhetoric, and the lack of interest shown by some of her more doctrinaire mentors, Heseltine's presence in the city convinced many of the locals that the Tory government cared.

At Westminster his progress was observed with a blend of cynicism and admiration. Some, with an eye to Heseltine's apparent ambition, saw it as another step towards Downing Street. Senior Tories like Willie Whitelaw who had long held doubts, disliked the adulation with which the media had come to report his activities. 'It was one long, bloody Heseltine conference speech', was the view of a cabinet colleague. Socialists, brought up to dislike his flamboyance, and strongly disapproving of his policies of retrenchment at the department of the environment, determined to give him no public credit. But there was no gainsaying the admiration of professional politicians for a bravura performance. Westminster takes some time to convince; the public, on the other hand, who had regarded him as a spectacular lightweight, with a taste for theatrics such as the mace affair, were bowled over. It was the breakthrough for which Michael Heseltine had been looking.

The more curmudgeonly politicians, especially on the Left, believed that Heseltine was simply protecting himself from the taint of opprobrium to which the government's 'uncaring' policies had given rise. And there was no sign of any additional money being made available by the treasury. The regional officer of the Trades Union Council, Colin Barnett, said, 'An end of term report would be "Superb ability to listen, doubtful facility with funds." He listens extraordinarily well, but whether he has any influence upon the Prime Minister or the chancellor is a matter for conjecture. The sense of alienation and frustration which would arise in all sections of the community on Merseyside if all this turns out wrong, will be tremendous.'

Some in Liverpool maintained that he had spent his time seeing the wrong people in the wrong order, and pointed to his refusal to visit Upper Parliament Street, where the violence had started, on the first day of his three-week visit. The police had advised against. The more radical, who had sought the head of the chief constable, Kenneth Oxford, were piqued by Heseltine's desire to keep police responsibility firmly where it belonged – with the home secretary, William Whitelaw. It is true that had the chief constable been sacked, tension would have been swiftly reduced, particularly in Toxteth. Yet, leaving aside the injustice of such a move, its effect upon police morale would have been devastating.

Michael Heseltine's frequent pleas to local businessmen to make room for more local jobs cut little ice. Several explained their inability or unwillingness to respond by asserting that even with two and a half million unemployed in Britain, Merseyside, recession or no recession, was effectively at full employment. The out of work were the unskilled; what Liverpool businessmen were looking for was the skilled, 'the sort who are giving up factory work to become milkmen and drivers'. And the government was doing 'nowt' to provide them. As with nearly everywhere else in the country, the service industries were gaining as manufacturing industry steadily declined. The plight of Liverpool, they pointed out, was no worse than the plight of Birmingham and the Black Country; but of course the riots at Handsworth were four years in the future.

The Heseltine approach was based on a partnership between the public and private sectors. Indeed, he argued against a grand strategy to reverse economic decline. What

84

was needed, he maintained in 1983, was a revival of the opportunities formerly created by cities. 'The momentum of events stimulated inner-city life. People were attracted to these despite the quite appalling conditions that prevailed. Somehow we have to recreate that sense of attraction and in circumstances where, rightly, people are far more discriminating about the quality of the environment in which they are prepared to live,' he said in a speech in 1986.

So far, so good. Can Britain's cities look to the return of the middle class which has fled them for exurbia? Only if land and houses are made available. But the evidence still points to a continuing flight from the cities, prompted in part by street crime and burglaries, or by exaggerated reports of their incidence. Only the Asian community with its entrepreneurial flair, promises regeneration. And government economic policies have, consciously or not, favoured the South while the Midlands and the North have declined in relative terms. Heseltine was correct when he asserted 'past opportunities were not the result of a masterplan. They were the product of uncoordinated decisions arising from our commercial and manufacturing prowess.' We are no further forward.

At the end of August 1981 Heseltine presented his own proposals on inner-city policy to the cabinet, a tendentious paper cheekily entitled 'It took a riot'. Its key recommendations included: cabinet ministers to be given individual responsibility for specific run-down areas; a new central government directorate in each inner-city area to be set up to coordinate state spending; a massive cut in the powers of the metropolitan councils which were blamed for wasting resources, and a new official committee in London, its task to ensure that any additional public spending was directly related to private sector projects.

Mrs Thatcher was reported to have reacted favourably to this manifesto, but second thoughts prompted by the treasury – Geoffrey Howe believed it to be no more than a well-disguised blank cheque – were much more cautious. She was torn between the need to adopt policies which gave a vivid impression of care and concern and the necessity, as she saw it, of maintaining a tight hold over public spending. She was hugely unpopular at the time, but she had no wish to concede defeat in what had been a long-drawn-out and bitterly fought battle that summer over public expenditure. Her colleagues, who were still chary of Heseltine's motives, and probably a touch jealous of his fame, dragged their feet. And which cabinet minister, up to his eyes in the minutiae of his departmental responsibilities, would welcome the additional burden of 'doing a Heseltine' himself on behalf of a city which he had never visited?

As is the case in politics, the agenda changed, and the Heseltine proposals were left to gather dust. Only had Toxteth burnt again would they have risen, phoenix-like, from the ashes of Liverpool 8. Nevertheless, Heseltine's viceroyalty was not a waste of time.

Peter Riddell, who is perhaps the most thoughtful political commentator of them all, wrote a summing-up in his book *The Thatcher Government*, from which I will quote:

Apart from the specifically Merseyside initiatives, there have been a variety of similar urban schemes. For instance, there has been a derelict-land grant (amounting to thirty million pounds initially) to secure the immediate development by private companies, with two hundred million pounds of investment, of land reclaimed by local authorities, and an urban development grant to assist projects involving a large input of private finance (forty million pounds at first). In addition, the government has encouraged the growth of local enterprise agencies and has set up urban development corporations to help regenerate the docklands of London and Merseyside. There has been much merit in these various partnership ideas, but the critics have a point in arguing that the £270,000,000 spent by the government in support of the urban programme in 1982–3 was dwarfed by the cutback in the rate support grant for many inner-city authorities.

There lies the rub, although, to be fair to Heseltine, his spending was directed at projects which were designed to rejuvenate, while the depleted rate support grant was destined to be spent in large part on welfare.

Today Heseltine's reputation in Liverpool stands high. David Fletcher, who is today the leader of the Wirral Borough Council, and a Tory, when asked whether Heseltine's three weeks had been worthwhile, answered 'very much so'. His initiative should serve 'as a model for the future'. Fletcher accompanied Heseltine when Michael paid a return visit to Merseyside in April 1986. One of Fletcher's tenants said that Michael had done more for this area than anyone else, an opinion which 'was repeated endlessly'. I asked Fletcher for examples of Heseltine's efforts to which Liverpudlians, and others, could point. The Woodchurch Estate in the Wirral, where Heseltine set up a deal with Wimpeys to renovate a postwar housing estate prior to selling many of the houses to their tenants, is one example of his efforts. Marconi has been encouraged to set up a high-tech. centre in the Wirral, and Cammell Laird, the Birkenhead shipbuilders, were not forgotten when Michael moved on to the ministry of defence. He ordered a frigate to be built at the yard, once thirty-seven striking crane drivers had been dismissed.

On the other side of the Mersey, Fletcher drew attention to the renovation of the Albert Dock, the site of the annual Garden Festival, and the setting-up by Heseltine of a group to monitor sites in the public sector so that they might be identified with a view to their sale and development. Many hopes rest with that body.

When asked to name his greatest achievement on Merseyside, Michael himself did not hesitate. 'The cleaning up of the River Mersey itself.' This attempt to cleanse what has become a sewer running between the port of Manchester and the Irish Sea has only just begun, and will take, according to Heseltine, till the end of the century. It could be that the Mersey salmon will become his most abiding memorial.

That October Michael Heseltine made what was undoubtedly his finest conference speech. He must have arrived in Blackpool, that windy city, which has turned its back on England, feeling on the crest of the wave. He had in the previous twelve months sprung into national prominence; he had become a household name. His foray on Merseyside had provided a battered government with a tangible political success. The Tory Party was full of rumour to the effect that certain unnamed senior figures would, before long, take the Prime Minister by the elbow and tell her that enough was enough. Her popularity ratings in the polls were the lowest of any prime minister since the war (they were to be almost as low in the autumn of 1986), and the standing of her government was little higher. The quarrels within the party and the expulsion of the 'wets' from her cabinet had upset the party faithful. And although it was not widely known at the time, her applause for every speaker from the floor who called for the return of hanging precipitated an unholy row with her home secretary, Willie Whitelaw, whose task it was to reply to the debate. 'I have been loyal to you through thick and thin,' he told Mrs Thatcher, 'and I expect as much in return.'

Heseltine, as might be expected, recounted the story of Liverpool. But he did more. He rubbed the powdered noses of his five thousand strong audience in the realities of the world beyond the hall. He warned them not to judge the deprived by our own standards (thus cutting across Mrs Thatcher's addiction to the beliefs of Samuel Smiles). 'We have to be very careful before we assume strengths and values in those deprived societies that are characteristic of a more vibrant and richer community elsewhere. Self-help has a limited meaning in an inner-city community where 40% of the kids may be without work, and if they are black the figure may be 60%. There is one labour exchange in central Liverpool where twenty thousand unemployed people are registered. Eight hundred youngsters applied to just one firm for thirty apprenticeships.'

The hall sat silent as Heseltine continued. 'We must realise the scale of the impact of concentrated unemployment, the hopelessness that it creates, the destruction of self-respect in every age group. We have to be very sure that we understand the attitudes of children to the authority of parents in a community where there are no prospects for many middle-aged people ever to work again.' Not since Mrs Thatcher had become leader of the party had Conservatives been spoken to in that way.

'Like Geoffrey Howe, I, too, come from South Wales. This nation (Wales) is still suffering from the legacies, from the folklore and from the memories of those bitter interwar years. They have fuelled a venom in the Labour Party and the trade unions that has set back our industrial society almost beyond redemption'.

Not content with a recital of home truths about employment, Heseltine went on to talk about immigration – but not before paying tribute to Disraeli's concept of One Nation. He did not stop there; he paid an extravagant tribute to the memory of Iain Macleod, regarded by many of the moderate Tories as the party's lost leader. There were few who could not break the code, which had masked the disputes within government and party. It was his most outspoken attack on Thatcherism.

'We talk of equality of opportunity. What do these words actually mean in the inner cities today? What do they mean to the black communities? We now have large immigrant communities in British cities. Let this party's position be absolutely clear. They are British. They live here. They vote here. However tight the immigration legislation – and in everyone's interest it should be tight – there will be a large black community in this country tomorrow, just as there is today. There are no schemes of significant repatriation that have any moral, social or political credibility.'

This was telling them. It was not so long since Mrs Thatcher had spoken on television of the country being 'swamped' by immigrants. Heseltine's audience of party activists probably share a sense of unease when confronted with the consequences of immigration; but by the same token, good manners serve to moderate their behaviour. There was, and is, an ill-mannered minority. The attitudes of the Conservative Party do not differ from those held by the public at large; and it could be asserted that the working-class Labour voter is even more hostile to the idea of colour, and to the presence of black neighbours. What is essential is that our leaders set a good example in racial matters. Michael Heseltine cannot be faulted on that account.

Heseltine ended his speech with the customary party political knockabout, poking fun at Denis Healey's recent observation that 'the real problem is to make Earth as much like Heaven as we can'. His view of the Social Democrats who had just sprung from the body of the Labour Party, bears repetition. 'It is the oldest story in the world. If you cannot sell the product change the wrapping. It is yesterday's mutton dressed up as tomorrow's mutton.' There was sugar on the pill. But there could be no doubt, as the conference stood to give him his usual standing ovation, that he had made them swallow it. For five minutes more, Heseltine was indeed the lord of all he surveyed.

Ruler of the Queen's Navee

On 6 January 1983 Mrs Thatcher announced Michael Heseltine's much-trailed appointment as secretary of state for defence. While no surprise, the appointment was nevertheless startling in its implications. Heseltine had never shown the slightest interest in the subject; foreign and security policies were to him a closed book. He was, however, a committed 'European', having never wavered in his support for Britain's entry into the Community. 'High' politics were considered to be not his scene; he was a practitioner of the 'low', that is the more mundane matters of the environment, business and the economy. Why then was he chosen?

There can be little doubt that Mrs Thatcher wanted him out of the way. His task, as she saw it, was to bend his energies towards reforming the ministry of defence, the second biggest spender, after health and social security, of public money. A Heseltine at work reorganising the ministry along the lines foretold by the Macmillan/Thorneycroft/Mountbatten 'reforms' of 1964, introducing MINIS and getting value for money in terms of defence procurement, would be a sensible exploitation of Heseltine's managerial talents. His appointment, which was designed to be of a long duration, would also have the undeniable advantage from Mrs Thatcher's point of view of removing a thorn in her side in terms of domestic politics. In early 1983 the Lady was not yet for Turning; the control of public spending was still the centrepiece of the government's economic strategy, and regional policy (as Michael had discovered) an anathema. Heseltine was clearly not suited to trade and industry. As an interventionist he would bring too much relish and public money to the job. Defence would keep Heseltine occupied, and largely out of Mrs Thatcher's hair.

It was a happy and exploitable coincidence that Michael Heseltine happened to be the best man to deal with the Campaign for Nuclear Disarmament. He is preeminently a communicator. The decision to deploy cruise missiles as a consequence of a decision taken in 1979, and at the insistence of the Nato Council, to serve as a counter to the rising number of Soviet intermediate range ballistic missiles, the SS20s, had encouraged the nuclear disarmers to mount a vociferous campaign. The Labour Party under Michael Foot's leadership had apparently adopted the policies of nuclear disarmament. The extent to which Labour became vulnerable to a Tory counterattack on the issues of defence can be simply demonstrated: the Conservative victory in the June 1983 general election was to a great extent due to Labour's vulnerability over defence. Heseltine's role was third only to General Galtieri's ambitions and Mrs Thatcher's determination to resist them, in the achievement of victory.

But this is to anticipate. On 6 January Heseltine packed his bags and moved over to the ministry of defence building in Whitehall, a massive and imposing building which owes much of its architectural inspiration to Albert Speer. The Orpen portrait of Lloyd George, of course, went with him, which should have served the generals as a warning. Had Heseltine paid more attention while at Pembroke to his political history tutor, Ronald McCallum, he would have remembered the bitter hostility between Lloyd George and the top brass in the Great War. The Generals had little time for the 'frocks' as they dubbed the frock-coated politicians, and none whatsoever for Lloyd George. A secretary of state with a better knowledge of history than Heseltine, and who wished to send a signal of his intent, might have made room on his walls for a second portrait, that of Leslie Hore-Belisha. In the event, Heseltine pinched Churchill's furniture which had once graced the admiralty, and proceeded to make himself comfortable.

He was made welcome by his private office. The permanent secretary was Sir Clive Whitmore, successor to the genial and very shrewd Frank Cooper; his private secretary, a young high-flying civil servant called Richard Mottram. The bureaucrats recognised Michael as a 'serious politician', an accolade which is sparingly awarded, and almost the highest form of Whitehall praise. He looked like, and sounded like, a cabinet minister, at a time when the cabinet, dominated by an imperious prime minister, seemed a refuge for nonentities. Heseltine, it was decided, had style, a certain aura. And, committed as they were to the defence of NATO, and of collective security, they were in search of a champion.

Heseltine also 'knew what he wanted'. Contrary to the impression given by Messrs Lynn and Jay, Whitehall is not full of Sir Humphrey Applebys. Top civil servants, especially in the ministry of defence, recognised that much needed to be done, and welcomed the innovator. MINIS may or may not have been 'a load of nonsense', but the reorganisation of the ministry itself, the 'defeat of CND' and getting value for money in the purchase of arms, were certainly not nonsensical objectives. If these problems were to be tackled, the civil servants, and even the Generals, would be prepared to submit cheerfully to humiliation through the compilation of charts.

Heseltine 'had his own agenda', and this was good news. Those who worked closely with him, over a period of almost three years, agreed that he was a very private person. A man who kept his own counsel. Some complained of never getting to know him properly. The staff at the ministry of defence is much larger than that at the department of the environment. There are in Whitehall approximately 160 senior people above the rank of rear admiral or its civilian equivalent. The Christmas parties which were such a feature of life at Marsham Street were not carried over to the ministry of defence. It was noted that Heseltine was not as clever as his predecessor, John Nott, and was no intellectual, but he was universally regarded as intelligent, shrewd and determined. He definitely was not 'an IISS man', that is, a devotee of the arcane mysteries of strategy (an art described by von Clausewitz as 'simple but not easy'). The International Institute for Strategic Studies in London is the home of strategy buffs to whom the complexities of deterrence have been made simple. I doubt if Michael had ever heard of Herman Kahn, let alone read him. But secretaries of state are not obliged to sit at the feet of the likes of Professor Sir Michael Howard, although it would be advantageous were they to do so.

I suppose the most cerebral of Heseltine's predecessors at the ministry of defence was Denis Healey, who had a taste for strategic studies and actually understood the 'theology' of deterrence. He travelled the world from conference to conference, a congenial activity common to strategists who make certain that the venues for their deliberations are situated either high up in the Alps or low on the shores of the Adriatic. Peter Carrington, secretary of state in Edward Heath's government, although no intellectual, was well regarded, being awarded high marks by both civilians and soldiers. Francis Pym was a traditional Tory, while John Nott was anything but. Nott's brave attempt at rationalisation, an exercise for which the Royal Navy would have been the sacrifice, foundered upon the noisy opposition of the Conservative back bench, and upon the Argentinian invasion of the Falklands. Having enjoyed a rough passage and a 'good' war, Nott called it a day, and finally did what he had long threatened to do, that is, to divide his time between his Cornish farm and the more profitable pastures of the City of London. His going gave Mrs Thatcher the opportunity to move Heseltine into defence.

The Lloyd George portrait was not the only thing Heseltine brought from the department of the environment. John Stanley came with him as well. Stanley is an immensely assiduous minister and no stranger to unpopularity. His task was to man the castle's gate. He absorbed detail like blotting paper and kept suppliant civil servants who wished to carry on exercising their right of access to the secretary of state, cooling their heels in the corridor. Stanley also served to keep Heseltine's colleagues on the Tory back benches at bay.

Heseltine's appetite for hard work became immediately apparent. He has been likened to 'a great steam engine', the furnace of which stood in need of frequent replenishment. He wanted 'a hot meal at lunchtime', a requirement that went unbegrudged. As at the department of the environment, he was capable of working consistently from 8.30 in the morning until the early evening, and then of taking up some boring political task, his civil servants having retired home to an early bed.

If Michael's private office approved of their new master, the senior serving officers, the generals, admirals and air marshals had their doubts. There was, they feared, something unsound about the secretary of state. Some believed he had not wanted the job in the first place; others pointed to his lack of knowledge or even interest in the subject. The suspicion with which some at least of the top brass regarded him was a factor of the conventionality which is the hallmark of senior serving officers. Competent, intelligent but somewhat narrow in outlook, the 'Generals' looked askance at a man they thought a careerist, whose ambition they recognised, but whose credentials they did not. A hairdresser at a fashionable London club has been reported as saying that a gentleman's hair has increased in length by at least an inch over the past ten years. This may well be true of stockbrokers but not of soldiers. The length of Heseltine's hair was a matter of much disapproval. A very senior soldier indeed told me with some relish a story of Heseltine in Germany inspecting some unit, anxious not to stand with his back to the Teutonic wind lest his hair be blown over his eyes, and spoil the view for the press photographers.

The products of Wellington and Sandhurst had to be convinced of the worth of a product of Shrewsbury and

Pembroke College, Oxford. The suits were just a shade too well cut, the ties too kipperish and the style too flash. The fact that Heseltine frequently wore a brigade tie served only to remind them of Michael's rather curious term as a national serviceman in the Welsh Guards. Hadn't the feller wangled an early discharge by begging leave to fight a hopeless Labour seat in the depths of Wales? I once asked a grenadier general whether he objected to Michael's wearing a brigade tie. 'Not in the least,' he replied, 'but I wish the chap wouldn't always tie it in a Windsor knot.'

Heseltine certainly had his ups and downs with the chief of the general staff, Field Marshal Sir 'Dwin' Bramall, and was sometimes found guilty of keeping officers hanging around for appointments; but he did manage to overcome most of the gut hostility with which he was greeted by senior servicemen. Senior officers have a fixed attitude towards secretaries of state. They approve of socialists who turn out (in their eyes) to be patriots, e.g. Shinwell and Healey. They strongly approve of gents-who-know-their-stuff, like Lord Carrington, and gents who defer, like George Younger. They do not, however, like difficult customers like John Nott, armed with a mind of his own, or like Michael Heseltine, who saw his task as being to knock heads together. But as decent men with a job to do they can be favourably impressed. Their initial judgements are soluble in achievement.

The first task of a newly appointed minister, at whatever level, is to read himself in. It cannot have been easy for Heseltine, uncomfortable with the written word, and ignorant of defence matters, to have made himself the master of his subject. His private office would undoubtedly have prepared papers for him and organised a series of briefings by experts. But Michael did his homework. His expertise, however, was later to be demonstrated only in certain fields. He could make the case against unilateral nuclear disarmament, although he was careful not to debate publicly on the same platform with his opponents. This was less a sign of a lack of intellectual self-confidence than a wary realisation that it was always a mistake to give a platform to one's opponents. He became an expert in matters of defence procurement, and he pursued the goals of European cooperation with zeal. He set his ministry to work discovering, via MINIS, what it was they were supposed to be doing. He was good on television and in the House, and he took care to cultivate the officers of the Conservative Party's Defence Committee with whom he would hold fortnightly meetings in his room in the House on 'battleship row', the name given to the large, cavernous, and for the most part empty, private rooms allocated to cabinet ministers within the Palace of Westminster. What he never became was an expert on the more esoteric matters such as 'flexible response', 'no first use' and minimum deterrence. Michael Heseltine is an executive not an academic.

Heseltine's reading, prepared by his staff, would have included a position paper, its purpose to instruct the tyro in matters of defence policy. It would have begun by explaining Britain's membership of the North Atlantic Treaty. The military organisation, that is, all the countries of Western Europe, save Spain, and not including France which, since de Gaulle, had remained a member of the Atlantic Alliance but not of the NATO military organisation, contributed land, sea and air forces to the defence of the East/West border. Greece and Turkey are two other Eastern European member states of the Alliance. The purpose of NATO, founded in 1948, is to link the United States to the defence of Europe as a means of discouraging Russian territorial ambitions. To that end Britain contributes fifty-five thousand troops, the British Army of the Rhine, which was stationed in northern Germany. We also contribute the 2nd Tactical Airforce, and the bulk of the Royal Navy for NATO duties in the North Sea, the Channel, and the Eastern Approaches. Membership of NATO dates from the days of Clement Attlee and Ernest Bevin. All political parties in Britain are in favour of our membership.

While the United States was the strongest power in the Alliance, Great Britain sustained several different, and expensive roles. Besides our NATO contribution, there was the defence of the homeland, a notional capacity for intervention, 'out of area', that is outside Europe, and the maintenance of our independent nuclear deterrent, which was the function of the Polaris squadron of the Royal Navy. The Army had a range of small, so-called battlefield nuclear weapons, the Royal Navy had nuclear depth charges, and the Royal Air Force was equipped with nuclear bombs. We thus bore a range of responsibilities which was more extensive than any other of our allies save for the United States.

To the cost of the above had been added the expense of the Falklands garrison, and of constructing an airfield there capable of taking long-range aircraft. None of these many commitments could be dispensed with. The question before the secretary of state was whether any of them could be discharged less expensively, for the pressures upon the defence budget, despite a 3% real increase in spending each year, were intense. The payment of an all-volunteer force, at rates which compared favourably with earnings in civilian life, was the most expensive system of military service, but the reintroduction of conscription had been judged to be politically unacceptable.

While it is not true that defence had suffered more from inflation than the rest of the government services – over the period 1973 to 1983, central government prices went up by 15.6%, slightly more than defence, and from 1980 to 1983 by 9.5%, exactly the same as defence – what pushes up defence costs is the very rapid rise in prices for the latest weapons and equipment. It is really only in common procurement, and then only if every opportunity is taken for joint production with our European partners, that any real possibility of savings lies.

So much so far makes up a child's guide to the problems of defence. Many commitments, scarce resources, pressures on costs, and growing public anxieties about the wisdom, and the morality, of relying upon nuclear weapons. A more sophisticated note could well have been slipped into Heseltine's nightly red box, that badge of office and satchel combined. The note would have made the point that the size of the British defence effort had at least as much to do with keeping the Americans in Europe as it had with keeping the Russians out. The American strategic nuclear guarantee had been eroded by Soviet prowess in nuclear weapons; but the presence in the line of the US 7th Army in Bavaria is the vital token of America's commitment to our mutual defence.

Since 1968 the foreign and commonwealth office had left defence policy to the ministry of defence. Heseltine's private office would have pointed out to him, in the course of his education, the fact that one of the inconveniences was that, while the foreign relations of Britain and its means of defence become steadily more complicated, the vast majority of electors, whose votes determine the choice of their rulers, cannot possibly have the knowledge necessary to understand the pros and cons of the various alternative policies on offer.

A substantial minority of the intelligentsia, however, is knowledgeable in this field. It includes, of course, the staff of the government departments concerned, the product of the major universities, the membership of institutions specialising in the study of international affairs, people experienced in diplomacy and the armed forces, and in the technology of modern armament, as well as experts on the economy.

Then there is a wide outer ring, as it might be called, of people who combine partial knowledge of these matters with a variety of political enthusiasms about them. The national policies which emerge from a general election are largely the result of the effect of this 'politicised intelligentsia' upon the general public. In combatting the Campaign for Nuclear Disarmament, Heseltine had to convince the public at large by demonstrating that the arguments of some at least of the outer ring of the political classes who had taken up the cause of unilateral disarmament were unsound.

In the first instance, the waxing of support for CND was, as I have already suggested, due to the decision to deploy cruise missiles in response to what was perceived to be a growing Soviet military and political threat. 'Détente', so fashionable in the 'seventies, had disappeared, to be replaced by the invasion of Afghanistan and a somewhat strident anti-Soviet rhetoric adopted by President Reagan and echoed by Mrs Thatcher. This rise in tension convinced a growing number that nuclear war was inevitable. But there were also other factors which served to stimulate opposition to orthodoxy in matters of defence.

Since the end of Hitler's War the foreign and defence policies of successive British governments had remained the same. That was because there existed, if only from force of habit, a common appreciation of the particular danger which had originally called the system of collective defence and security into being. This appreciation was fortified by a distinctive patriotic tradition. All this had found its place for a lifetime within the North Atlantic Alliance.

During this period there had been no war in Europe. This prolonged peace, almost unprecedented in European history, made it hard to convince the intelligentsia and the general public that armed vigilance was necessary, and still harder to explain the vital part played by nuclear weapons in deterring the Soviet Union from embarking upon war or adventure. The change in NATO strategy in favour of 'flexible response' (which implied the first use of allied nuclear weapons in the event of the defeat of NATO's conventional forces) in 1967, came eventually to be regarded by some as an unsatisfactory and dangerous departure. But as we have seen, it was not until the 1979 decision to deploy cruise and Pershing missiles in Europe that public controversy was set ablaze.

Thus, there had been building up since 1979, the year in which, coincidentally, Mrs Thatcher came to power, a political agitation of a quite remarkable dimension. The political consensus on defence had been breached, and in consequence the nuclear disarmament campaigns of the 'fifties and 'sixties were revived. In a valedictory article as secretary-general of NATO, Joseph Luns wrote in April 1984, 'We have indeed been witnessing a healthy repoliticisation of the entire discussion of the East/West relationship.' A good example, perhaps, of Dutch understatement.

To meet the challenge of the nuclear disarmers, Heseltine set up a special unit within the ministry of defence called DS19. It was a task well suited to his talents. His predecessor, John Nott, had not been perceived either by Mrs Thatcher or her advisors as a man with the necessary public presence to enable him to cope. DS19 was given a staff of seven, and placed under the control of Mr John Ledlie, an assistant secretary. The unit's tasks included helping Heseltine with his speeches and newspaper articles, and preparing films, pamphlets and leaflets setting out the case for nuclear weapons. It was to deal directly with the press on the nuclear issue, collate the findings of public opinion polls, and handle the publicity aspect of demonstrations mounted against Heseltine by the CND. An idea of an advertising campaign, handled by J. Walter Thompson, had been floated in the past. Heseltine set his face against it. The budget for DS19 was officially described as a 'shoestring'. Starved or not, the unit proved to be highly effective.

Just how effective can be shown by two sets of figures: a MORI survey in January 1983 showed 54% of those polled to be opposed to cruise missiles; a poll in late May showed 52% in favour. Polling day for the general election determined early in May was on 9 June.

In an attempt to build on their success in October 1981, when an estimated one hundred and fifty thousand people took part in a demonstration against nuclear weapons (the largest ever), CND had organised several similar demonstrations. Some thirty thousand women demonstrated at Greenham Common in December 1982. Over the Easter weekend 1–4 April 1983 several demonstrations, attracting tens of thousands, were held across the country. An estimated forty thousand people held hands to form a 'chain' that stretched seventeen miles from the proposed missile base at Greenham Common, via the nuclear weapons plant at Aldermaston, to another plant at Burghfield. All this activity resulted in a very great deal of publicity, a large proportion of which was sympathetic. Heseltine's DS19 had no time to lose.

Heseltine made it a cornerstone of his strategy never to debate with CND. He refused a television confrontation, preferring to cross swords only with the Labour Party. As we have seen, he was chary of giving Bruce Kent and Joan Ruddock yet another platform, but there was more to his refusal than that. Labour MPs were elected representatives, responsible to the voter at an election; the Campaign for Nuclear Disarmament was a pressure group, responsible to no one save its left-wing dominated executive committee. He would refute their arguments in a series of public meetings and interviews: when he had done so, the Labour Party would be obliged to pay the price for any diminution in support of unilateral, or 'one-sided' disarmament. It was a clever tactic, and one that worked.

The public were spectators at a gladiatorial contest. It was not exclusively, however, between Heseltine and his two principal opponents, Kent and Ruddock; Tory MPs were first discouraged, and then encouraged, by Central Office to meet the CND in public debate. The Tory whips, happy to come between man and wife as a general rule, waved members of their pack away from Westminster with a new liberality. I debated against Bruce Kent in Reading before a packed town hall, and later took on Joan Ruddock in the Oxford Union. Of the two, I found Joan Ruddock the more difficult opponent. She was articulate, quiet-voiced and moderate; too many Tories, I suspect, believed that they could blow her out of the water. They could not. The 'turbulent priest' was a softer touch. But we were the foot soldiers; the campaign against the Campaign was led from the front by an embattled Michael Heseltine.

As he turned the tide, so his opponents' hostility towards him grew. He was daubed with paint by protesting women, and jostled coming out of a meeting in Newbury. Heseltine's assertion that CND was a left-wing organisation does not seem to have gone beyond the bounds of decency. There *were* Communists on its executive, though they were a minority. The cry of 'smear' was, I believe, a bogus one. After all, the Campaign for Nuclear Disarmament would find it hard to deny, then or now, that most of its members are left-wing, where 'left' is defined as someone broadly sympathetic to the Labour Party rather than to the Tories. All Heseltine did was to point out, perfectly legitimately, that most of the members were in fact left-wing. Some wanted Britain to stay in a non-nuclear NATO; others wanted Britain to be neutral in the context of the cold war; still others would have had us change sides in the East/West conflict. Like the political parties, CND is a left-wing coalition in continual debate.

The Cathy Massiter affair was, on the surface, more sinister; but on examination, Heseltine can be absolved of any blame. Ms Massiter worked for MI5, where she had been employed checking up on the activities of members of the campaign. Heseltine made use of this information as political ammunition. He was well within his rights to do so, although had Heseltine actually instructed her to work within MI5 to obtain discreditable information, this would have exposed him to legitimate criticism. But he did nothing of the kind, he simply made capital out of information which was already available.

Heseltine shares the politician's hunger for publicity, and his campaign against the 'ban the bombers' brought him before the public as never before. He seemed to be never off the telly. He was very effective at presenting policies and issues. While he did not really understand several of the key issues in the deterrent argument, he knew enough about them to convince the public. He stumbled only once, at Molesworth.

Molesworth is an obscure Cambridgeshire village whose airfield was chosen as the second cruise missile base. Ringed by demonstrators, Heseltine led a relieving force of soldiers and police. He was driven to the base in his black ministerial Rover, cocooned from the rain. Secretaries of state live privileged lives. While they no longer have valets as Lord Curzon had Arketall, they have the members of their private office. They are brought and fetched, picked up and carried. The idea of taking a coat to the wet and windy fastnesses of rural East Anglia, or at the very least a Chamberlainite umbrella, did not occur to Heseltine. Hence, on his arrival at the base, shivering in the rainy dark, a solicitous senior army officer handed him a flak jacket. 'Why ruin a good suit, Minister?' Why, indeed.

The photographs of Michael looking for all the world as if he were the head of state of some banana republic, girdled the world, and gave much pleasure to his friends and even more comfort to his enemies. 'General' Heseltine had clearly won the 'Battle of Molesworth' and against a handful of bobble-hatted women. 'So what?' was his response, and he returned to London to play out his hand against CND with his customary care.

The general election of 1983 has become known, in retrospect, as 'the Falklands election'. A more accurate description might be 'the disarmer's election'. Defence, which had hitherto played no part whatever in general elections, since the policy had been bipartisan, thrust itself to the top of the agenda. The fact that we had just fought and won a war against the Argentine for the recapture of a group of small and largely uninhabited islands, served as a colourful back-drop to those who would make the 'patriotic' case.

By May, as we have seen, 52% favoured the stationing of cruise. In October of the same year 62% of the population favoured an East/West nuclear balance. (In a breakdown of this figure, it appeared that 50% of the Labour Party favoured this approach.) The Labour Party campaign document 'New Hope for Britain' outlined what the party hoped to accomplish during the lifetime of one parliament. This included a commitment to cancel the Trident programme and to reject the deployment of US cruise missiles. In addition, Labour promised to pursue 'a non-nuclear defence policy', including the removal from the United Kingdom of all existing US and UK nuclear bases and weapons. The document included the qualifying proviso that the intended nuclear disarmament would be undertaken with the consultation and cooperation of the NATO allies.

Relations between the Labour Party and the key element of the 'Peace Campaign', the CND, were strained during the election campaign, since unilateralists in both groups had to contend with an influential multilateralist contingent within the Labour Party. The CND policy of a complete withdrawal from NATO had been rejected by the Labour Party. The CND, in turn, was somewhat sceptical that Labour would, if elected, fully implement its defence policy. Thus Heseltine's decision to target the Labour Party paid off. Labour was not only perceived by the electorate as unreliable and unpatriotic, it was also seen to be split on the issue. With Labour's defeat, much of the heart went out of the Campaign for Nuclear Disarmament, and Michael Heseltine could claim the credit for a famous victory.

If the heart had gone out of the 'Peace Movement', the tail continued to twitch, as the arrival of the first American cruise missiles at Greenham Common drew near. Looking back, I think it plain that the campaign in favour of unilateral nuclear disarmament was, in fact, a phoney one. There was no more danger of nuclear war breaking out between the superpowers at that time than there had ever been since the construction of a balance of power between them. Nothing was less likely than the lurid pictures of the 'holocaust' with which CND threatened the Western world; nothing sillier than the 'nuclear-free zones' which some Labour local authorities solemnly instituted in order to demonstrate their superior concern. But, for a time, the campaign was able to exploit to the full the Christian and post-Christian anti-militarism endemic to Britain, West Germany and the Netherlands in particular. When, however, the British electorate, not normally interested in foreign affairs or in defence, woke up to the feeling that unilateral nuclear disarmament could leave the country defenceless, the result was a predictable loss of seats by Michael Foot's Labour Party.

After the Thatcher victory of 9 June 1983 Michael Heseltine returned in some triumph to the ministry of defence. His relations with the Prime Minister were, on the surface at least, correct. As we have seen, in the civil war that had raged throughout her first administration between 'wets' and 'dries', Heseltine had taken great care not to be publicly identified with Mrs Thatcher's enemies. His opposition to her economic policies was carried out solely within the cabinet. It is true to say that Heseltine, while in government, never once attempted to undermine Mrs Thatcher's authority to the media, a reticence which was in vivid contrast to other serving and one-time cabinet ministers who spoke of their disapproval and distaste in a code which was easily broken. Heseltine did not like her, or her style of government, but he bit his tongue.

In fact, he did more. While at the department of the environment Heseltine had once been faced with the prospect of a prime-ministerial tour of inspection. He took great pains to ensure that the visit went smoothly and to see that the department's views were conveyed to her in the most effective way. In an earlier departmental visit elsewhere there had been an occasion when the Prime Minister had been trapped in a lift for twenty minutes, during which her voice could be heard encouraging the mechanics. At the environment, Michael took great care to see that his lifts were in proper working order and manned. He even made discreet enquiries to discover what was her favourite food, which is chicken salad. He also stage-managed the departmental presentation, rehearsing a dozen senior civil servants in their allotted two and a half minutes each. As soon as one bureaucrat sat down, another stood up.

Only once, as far as I know, did the mask slip. I ran into Heseltine in the 'no' lobby of the Commons during a vote in the summer of 1983. I spoke of something Mrs Thatcher had said or done. 'That bloody woman,' was his reply. He had surprised himself. Immediately he pledged my silence, which I cheerfully gave. But four years later I am, as cheerfully, prepared to break it.

Mrs Thatcher was well aware of the fact that the ministry of defence had always been something of a backwater. She expected nonetheless that Heseltine would be kept fully occupied once the excitements of the general election and managing DS19 were behind him. He would immediately and inevitably have to cope with the pressures from the treasury to spend less, while under equal pressures from industry and the services to spend more. It has been said that Heseltine failed to resolve this dilemma, leaving the ministry overcommitted when he quit in January 1986.

Most politicians quickly become frustrated by having to protect their budgets from the depredations of the treasury. Ambitious ministers, and Heseltine in particular, are not in politics to consider spending levels. Politicians are happiest when talking, at their most miserable when making up their minds. And although Heseltine had a quick mind, he was not good at taking decisions. He soon won a reputation in Whitehall for putting things off. He would frequently take months to make up his mind.

Heseltine is an opportunist who is wary of bureaucracy. He discovered, as others have before him, that management in government is far harder than in private industry. At Haymarket, Heseltine had a staff of 611; at the ministry of defence there were six hundred thousand on the rolls. And in government there were so many more restraints. He was slow to take decisions because he found them genuinely difficult to make. He was cautious in the extreme, weighing the political consequences of each one with care. He knew that however good a decision may be, once taken, someone would always find fault with it. And that 'someone' would not be confined to the Opposition front bench. We all have a self-image of sorts; in Heseltine's case, it was of a platform politician of remarkable verbal skills and imposing presence, and, just as important, of a 'manager' who could convert his private success in building a business into the running of a government department. At environment he had combined public flair (Liverpool) with administrative competence, but the scale of activity at Marsham Street was much smaller. At defence, it fell to him to complete the process of internal reorganisation, begun under Harold Macmillan in the 'sixties. This has come to be seen by insiders as his principal achievement.

In fact Heseltine did not reorganise the ministry of defence as much as is widely believed. He carried forward the rationalisation begun by Lord Ismay and Sir Ian Jacob, continued under Macmillan by Thorneycroft and Mountbatten, and encouraged by Sir Solly Zuckerman; more still remains to be done.

Before Heseltine the ministry of defence was a loose confederation of groups, the three most obvious being the three armed services with their respective chiefs. Thus, with the existence of the chief of the defence staff, who was chosen on the principle of 'Buggins' Turn' from each of the services, there were four top military voices. There was a clear need to centralise and to coordinate decision-making. In the past defence decisions had all too often been taken after negotiation between the three heads of services. Each service had its pet project, and the other two agreed not to interfere with it on a reciprocal basis. The chief of the defence staff was thus presented with a fait accompli, which was often passed on to the ministers as 'agreed'. Some bad decisions were made. As one minister of state told a select committee: 'I cannot pretend that the machinery for taking the really big decisions is very sophisticated.' Another said, 'As minister for the Navy, I presided over a programme of procurement which I inherited and later passed on to my successor. We seldom paused to consider what we were doing or why we were doing it. As a minister, it was my job, and I admit it was my fault.' The admission was mistaken; it was not his fault, but the system's.

Thus, in theory, the interests of the three services were

supposed to be subsumed in an all-powerful fourth organisation at the centre of the ministry. 'What centre?' was the
comment of one of Heseltine's predecessors. And it is not too
long ago that a permanent secretary observed, 'If you want to
get anything done in this building, you pretty well have to do
it yourself.' There was never a lack of competing interests:
the Army, Navy and Air Force, the procurement executive,
and the industrial interest. This comparative lack of direction
had several consequences: the relative share of the budget as
between each service has been difficult to change; and the
primacy of the single service point of view tended to militate
against taking the difficult decision. What sailor would be
prepared to agree with the proposition that missiles would
make mincemeat of an Atlantic convoy, if his acquiescence
meant reducing the size of the surface fleet? No cavalryman
will admit that tanks are less effective against other tanks if
that means handing over the anti-tank role to the infantry.
No airman in the age of the missile will 'talk down' the role
of the manned aircraft. In short, for as long as the three
services played judge and jury in their own courts, no verdict
was ever in doubt.

During the 'seventies there was little progress towards a
solution of the problem. It could be argued that things got
worse. A former secretary of state, irritated by the activities
of one of his service ministers, was heard to say that he
thought those posts had been abolished. He was tactfully
reminded that they had been, but that he himself had restored
them.

Two factors served to bring things to a head. The cost of
weapons has been rising faster than that of inflation by
anything between 6% and 14%. In 1940 a Hurricane cost
seven thousand pounds; today an equivalent fighter aircraft
can cost twenty million pounds. Allowing for a tenfold fall in
the value of the pound, one of today's aircraft could purchase
three hundred forty-five years ago. Traverse the eye forward
and it would appear that in the year 2062 AD, we will be able
to afford only one combat aircraft. The price of a warship in

real terms doubles every five years. Officials call this phenomenon the 'road to absurdity'.

The other galvanising factor was the Falklands War. It was a close-run thing. Had the Argentinian bomb fuses all functioned properly, we might have lost sixteen warships and not six. We had the bad luck to lose four helicopters in transit, which left one heavy helicopter plus a captured Argentinian craft to move the entire Army. We were not equipped with weapons suitable for 'knocking out' airfields. There were other shortcomings, and although both the planning and execution of operations were superb, some people were reminded of Bernard Shaw's quip that the British serviceman can stand up to anything except the British war office. It should be remembered, however, that the task force was hastily cobbled together and drawn from all units – and fifteen years after the 1967 defence white paper had given a policy pledge to the effect that it was not the role of the armed forces to carry out opposed landings.

The three services had been moved into one building in 1963. Denis Healey set up the Programme Evaluation Group to monitor the competing claims of the three services, but the chiefs of staff emasculated it by the denial of information and by ridiculing its conclusions. In theory, at least, the Defence Council was the supreme authority; in practice, it seldom met save for the taking of group photographs.

Yet some progress had been made. Despite a tendency not to pose, let alone answer, difficult questions of inter-service priorities, the defence equipment budget rose over the ten years from 1973 to '83 from 33% to 46% – the highest percentage increase for any defence budget in the world. The ministry's basic failure was its lack of control over research and development.

Michael Heseltine was in charge of an organisation more than three times the size of the biggest private employer in the country. In 1983 six billion pounds were spent on new equipment, giving jobs to 220,000 people directly, and to about the same number indirectly. A further 140,000 jobs depended on the export of defence equipment. Heseltine was the primer of the nation's pump. To buy this equipment, the ministry signed thirty thousand separate contracts with industry. In 1981/2, the year before Heseltine was appointed, fifty-seven companies in Britain each got more than five million pounds worth of defence contracts; nine obtained more than one hundred million worth each.

The defence industries produce everything from nuclear submarines to space equipment. Defence orders in 1983 took more than 28% of the country's electronic output, almost 40% of its shipbuilding, and almost 50% of its aerospace production. In 1982 the Public Accounts Committee discovered that since 1980 some defence contractors may have made seventy-five million pounds a year in 'excess' profits. A lot of money, but seventy-five million is only 2.5% of the contracts placed annually in the early 'eighties. The scale of the problem facing Heseltine within the ministry can be demonstrated by one statistic: the enterprise was so vast that production orders worth less than fifty million pounds did not go to ministers for approval.

Heseltine laid siege to this citadel. He made use of four 'weapons': the appointment of Peter Levene at a salary of ninety thousand pounds a year, to be in charge of procurement; the reorganisation of the ministry itself, strengthening the centre at the expense of the various rival interests; the pursuit of wider European cooperation in weapons production; and MINIS.

One observer, hitherto a sceptic, was convinced of the value of MINIS when listening to a lecture by an admiral from the ship procurement department at Bath. A Second Sea Lord, who had taken the chair, summed up by saying that it had been a most illuminating talk. 'I have often wondered what went on at Bath,' he said.

Heseltine has said of MINIS, 'It is the only way I know in which the debates between ministers and the machine can be conducted on an equal basis.' Without these debates, he claimed, 'there was no detailed capacity for the people at the top to know what is happening.' So, the eighty individuals in defence management were subject to a catechism about their particular jobs. Each one was then interviewed, either by Heseltine or by an 'officer' of the special unit put in charge of the operation. Visiting MPs, such as the officers of the Tory Party's Defence Committee, were bewildered by a fresco of multi-coloured wall charts. Many bureaucrats, not surprisingly, complained of this inquisition; one replied that it was his ambition to be 'left alone'. Heseltine was heard to murmur that it was not the sort of reply with which parliament would feel satisfied, 'and, to be frank, neither would I'. The result was a pile of reports two feet high.

Some officials thought it all risible. They felt that the ministry was already overmanaged, and, what was more, MINIS would never reach far enough down to find anything of importance. Others had no doubt that he was right. 'The department is not a problem-solving machine,' said one, 'its function is to keep the show on the road. Civil servants do not want to change. They are a conservative bunch.' Heseltine himself explained, 'They'll all run themselves, given a chance . . . if you are not careful as a minister you can find yourself the titular head of the bureaucratic machine.'

Michael Heseltine looked for four things from MINIS: a reduction in overheads so as to leave more resources for the fighting units; managers made more accountable for their spending; more productive relations with industry on the basis of greater competition, and more efficient use of the ministry's considerable research capability.

The final touches to the master flow chart for the reorganisation proper were added to the back of an envelope during the flight home from a visit to Kuwait. It was typically 'Heseltine'. Sir Edwin Bramall (now Lord Bramall), the chief of the defence staff, was given only four days' warning, and two of those comprised a weekend. When later he was asked why, Heseltine replied, 'I could have gone through the process of producing a document worked out in considerable detail within the ministry which would have been made widely available within the building, and thus widely available outside. A leak would have created little short of an uproar . . .' Heseltine had decided to work with a small group of advisors only and to table finally what was essentially his plan.

Now John Nott had tinkered with the problem in 1981 when he made the chief of the defence staff his sole military advisor, but Heseltine in 1984 went much further. His aim was 'to simplify radically the present structure of the organisation of defence'. To that end the three separate services were brought under the umbrella of the chief of the defence staff, who would be responsible for the preparation and conduct of all military operations. The three service chiefs would be largely relieved of their policy-making functions, and reduced to managers of their own services. But they were permitted to retain their right of access to the prime minister. Policy was to be entrusted to an enlarged central staff, too powerful, it was hoped, to be ignored, as had happened to the Programme Evaluation Group. Most significantly, the Heseltine Plan (with the joint authorship, perhaps, of his permanent secretary Sir Clive Whitmore) coralled not only the operational requirement staffs but the most senior civilians into the new central, policy staff. This departure added a new storey to the process of structural reform.

The rationale for all these changes was the need to centralise and to coordinate decision-making. The broad themes centred around the belief that policy-making needed to be streamlined; that financial management needed strengthening, and that greater integration was needed between soldier and civilian. The reformers believed that there had been too many parallel hierarchies. Heseltine believed they should be fused together.

There was opposition, not least from the service chiefs, who found that they were no longer to be the makers of policy, but mere undermanagers in charge of their own backyards. On this matter Heseltine was forced to retreat. Each service was given a chief policy planner. But the service chiefs accepted subordination to the chief of the defence staff without a fight. The CDS, Field Marshal 'Dwin' Bramall, a clever soldier, took it in his stride. 'We'll just have to try to make it work,' was the gist of his Order of the Day.

Heseltine made the announcement of his reorganisation to parliament on 12 March 1984. In the aftermath of his statement, a steering group was set up under Sir Clive Whitmore, the PS. This consisted of Bramall, Admiral of the Fleet Sir John Fieldhouse, of Falklands fame and now the First Sea Lord, and Ewen Broadbent, the second permanent secretary. In due course the four chiefs, that is, including 'Dwin' Bramall the CDS, prepared a joint submission deploring the destruction of the three services' policy-making role. On receipt of this broadside, Heseltine suggested that the chiefs take advantage of their long-standing right of access to the prime minister. This they did, but, predictably, they came up against an immoveable object. Mrs Thatcher had not relished the revolt of the Royal Navy (and the support given to it by Keith Speed, the Navy minister) at the time of John Nott's defence review.

A short white paper went to parliament in the dog days of July. Heseltine had won. Three years before John Nott had had to fight for his political life in the face of Admiral Sir Henry Leach's opposition to Nott's proposed reductions in the size of the surface fleet. Leach was unashamedly committed to the defence of the Royal Navy. When Keith Speed was sacked by Margaret Thatcher for backing his service, the First Lords lined the steps of the ministry of defence building as a gesture of solidarity and farewell. The Navy lobby within the Tory Party flew the battle ensign and the party's seadogs, Sir Anthony Buck MP, a former Navy minister, and Sir Patrick Wall in particular, snapped at Nott's heels. Why then did Heseltine get away with it so easily?

I think it was because no one service could cry 'danger'. The Royal Navy had been spared the worst of Nott's reductions, and the arguments of economy and rationalisation which were deployed by the reformers under Heseltine were in tune with the party's mood. The officers of the party's Defence Committee were in favour of what Heseltine was trying to do; the bulk of the Tory backbenchers took their cue from them.

Heseltine's relations with 'Dwin' Bramall were generally good, though they had their ups and downs. Their principal disagreement was over punctuality. The field marshal had the soldier's obsession with time; Heseltine's approach to punctuality was more relaxed. The secretary of state had been known to keep very senior officers waiting in anterooms furnished only with a coathanger, pictures of passing clouds and elderly, tattered magazines, for over an hour. Driven to distraction by this discourtesy, the chief of the defence staff positioned on his desk a board proclaiming 'on call', which when waved at him by a functionary from Heseltine's private office, indicated that he (Bramall) should cancel all arrangements until further notice. It was noticed, however, that Heseltine's hair had become shorter and thus less outrageous. It was one of the few concessions Heseltine made.

Denis Healey in characteristic vein once defined the job of secretary of state for defence as a choice between being 'a twit or a bastard'. Heseltine has never been afraid to court unpopularity in a good cause. The Top Brass were really complaining of a loss of power to make decisions in the interest of their own service. The civil servants, too, had complaints to make. They did not like the idea of being fused into a centralised staff with military and civilian personnel being forced to work closely together. But they did not have the right of access to the prime minister. Heseltine has explained that he wanted to inject what he called 'creative tension' into the organisation. He did this by setting up a separate group consisting entirely of civil servants who were to be in charge of resources, and who were obliged to approve or challenge all spending proposals. This was the key element in what Heseltine was attempting to do.

He also felt that the Arms Control Group was not functioning properly, because it reported directly to the chief of the defence staff. Since no one would expect the CDS and the individual service chiefs to be in favour of arms control, Heseltine thought it essential that a separate group of civil servants should report directly to him on this issue. This reveals an interesting paradox. While widely perceived, and especially by the left-wing, as the arch enemy of CND, and as a fervent supporter of NATO, Heseltine actually spent a lot of time trying to feel his way towards a more constructive dialogue with the Russians. In this respect he is a 'détente man', falling comfortably into the 'wet' camp among Tories on foreign policy.

There was little subsequent consultation before vesting day on 1 January 1985. Officials claimed that there was as much time for discussion as there had been in John Nott's day, but the consultation resembled the trial of Blanco Posnet in Shaw's drama: 'You'll hang, Blanco, but we'll see you get a fair trial first.' In that spirit, there was more fulmination than deliberation. At one point the ministry claimed to defer to the views of former chiefs of the defence staff, but 'as they all said different things, we kept on course'.

Marshal of the RAF Lord Cameron and Admiral of the Fleet Lord Hill-Norton were highly critical of the reforms. Lord Cameron warned that the proposals would put the civil service and the military 'in a confrontation situation'. He continued, 'What happens when people are being killed because of bad decisions by the policy-making staff, because they have been insufficiently argued? Here we have power without responsibility, a recipe for disaster.' Some thought Cameron's hostility had been influenced by the passing over of the chief of the air staff, Air Marshal Williamson, as the next CDS, despite it being his 'turn'. Whatever his reasons, Cameron was not to be appeased. 'The removal of policy-making elements from the departments and denigrating the service chiefs is going too far. The chiefs become no more than glorified inspectors-general.'

Lord Hill-Norton said that the Heseltine Reforms would

be greatly resented by the armed forces. 'Raw commercial management techniques are inappropriate for dealing with men who might be asked to die in action.' But the dreadnoughts were not all on the same side. Field Marshal Lord Carver broadly welcomed the changes, as did Admiral of the Fleet Lord Lewin. The admiral particularly approved the movement towards closer integration between servicemen and civilians.

Michael Heseltine had thus created a strong, central machine, one that could ask questions like Marshall Foch's 'De quoi s'agit-il?' (What are you trying to achieve?) While it is, of course, vital to ask the right questions, what is perhaps more important is the evaluation of the answers received. The first may well have been achieved: as to the second, it is too early to tell. What is clear is that there can be no 'right' formula for arriving at the 'right' answers. Heseltine's Oberkommando der Wehrmacht (the 'OKW' of the German army in the Second World War) was the culmination of a series of attempts at reform, as I have already pointed out, the first of which was envisaged a quarter of a century earlier by those two brilliant soldiers, Generals Ismay and Jacob. One 'reform' remains necessary. George Younger, Heseltine's successor as secretary of state, has yet to find the revolutionary will to abolish the distinction between members of the three separate armed services over a certain rank. Ismay and Jacob argued that everyone over the rank of brigadier, senior captain and air commodore should be placed on a single promotion list. If they were not, they would carry their tribal prejudices to the very top. Younger is almost the ideal replacement for Heseltine. Decent, straightforward and less demanding, he has been careful to take his ministry out of the limelight. Had he brought a painting from the Scottish office with which to adorn his room overlooking the river, it would surely have been 'The Monarch of the Glen'.

The reorganisation carried out by Heseltine does not suggest that its creator was indifferent to policy. He may have been

117

no specialist but he was obsessed with its primacy. Heseltine is a conceptualiser, while Mrs Thatcher merely slaughters sacred cows. Heseltine has never been slow to spot the main political chance, whether it be Europe, state intervention in industry, the plight of the inner cities or the reorganisation of the ministry of defence. Having knocked up a new structure, Heseltine turned his attention to the problems of weapons procurement, both national and international.

It has been long regarded a truth that all defence ministries in Europe and America are 'ripped off by the defence equipment industries'. The quotation comes from a high official in the Pentagon. We have already seen the extent of the dependence of the British arms industry upon government orders, with the ministry of defence taking half the output of the British aerospace industry, and 40% of shipbuilding and repair work. And among their many successes have been startling failures, such as torpedoes, howitzers and the Nimrod early warning programme, the costs of which soared over budget and which Younger was obliged to cancel in favour of AWACS in December 1986 – incidentally this decision had Heseltine's support. The cost-plus contract did not encourage economy, but the high price to the taxpayer was all too often overlooked. The maintenance of a national defence industry capable of supplying (at a price) a full range of equipment for our armed services has long been considered a prerequisite of national sovereignty. Were economic efficiency and national sovereignty mutually exclusive? Many had thought them so.

One weapon employed by Michael Heseltine was competition. New principles were laid down. For example, a prime contractor was expected to introduce competition whenever possible in subcontracts. Competition should be introduced in the early stages of projects to widen the government's choices and to stimulate new ideas. This, it was hoped, would open the door to systems analysis: the ministry of defence simply states the operational requirement without insisting on any particular method of fulfilling it, and leaves the answer to those with sharp minds and technical expertise. And it was laid down that contractors developing a weapons system could no longer depend on getting the initial production orders, a right which some had come to regard as God-given.

But competition in the defence field comes up quickly against limits. It is never enough to rely upon the ideas of Adam Smith and Richard Cobden. The fact is that for most major weapons systems there is only *one* source of supply. Nearly all military aircraft and missiles come from British Aerospace: warships from British Shipbuilders, torpedoes from GEC Marconi, engines from Rolls-Royce and helicopters from Westland. Such is the complexity and cost of these weapons systems that companies have grown larger through amalgamation as the pressures both of governments and the marketplace have forced a more rational structure upon them. The alternative was to buy from abroad, a choice that was always politically very difficult to make. And production under licence of foreign designs robbed British industry of much of its virility. Why should the British taxpayer be asked to export employment when our home industries were crying out for orders? The principle of competition is all very well, but where does competion come from in high-cost projects, if not from abroad?

In times of vaulting costs, top priority must be given to the lengthening of production lines: hence the so-called 'European dimension'. In the mid-'seventies international political organisations like the Western European Union, set up in the early 'fifties to implement the Brussels Treaty of 1954 to which seven Western European countries had affixed their signatures, focused political attention upon the desirability of the joint European procurement of weapons. By the 'eighties everybody had come to know that European collaboration in procurement would make the most sense. It would lead to lower unit costs and to the standardisation of equipment within NATO which would save the taxpayers of Europe and America a fortune, and make the NATO forces more effective. Everybody knew it was the right course to take, if only it could be done.

Heseltine had long been attracted to a partnership with Europe; a partnership of equals. As long before as 1973, speaking in Los Angeles as minister for aerospace, he had said,

> For many years I have believed that for Britain and Europe the arguments lead overwhelmingly to the conclusion that . . . we would find it increasingly difficult to maintain an advanced industrial base unless we moulded together a partnership of nations that in total would be the equal of the competition to which the rest of the world would increasingly expose us. The resources of fifty million British people – however proud we may be of what we have achieved – never will in the future match across the spectrum the technologies and capabilities available to you, and one or two other major powers. Mounting costs of maintaining a technologic base and the lengthening lead times that are inseparable from today's achievements make it hard enough for a medium-sized nation even to maintain a relative position.

Was this his master's voice? The views were certainly those of the prime minister, Mr Edward Heath. But Heseltine continued, 'If you add the civil space budgets of Europe together, it emerges that we are spending approximately one sixth of the equivalent spent in the United States. But whereas you have one national agency, coordinating your total resources, we have not only competing national programmes but even fragmentation of expenditure within national boundaries.'

Eleven years later he returned to this theme. He told the Royal United Services Institute: 'A stronger Alliance depends ultimately upon a more equal industrial partnership. While the flow of arms exports from the US to Europe is less of a one-way street than it has been, it is still not good enough. In 1983 Europe's total population was 367,000,000 compared with 267,000,000 in the United States, but the GNP per head was only some seven thousand dollars compared with fourteen thousand for the United States.' He deplored the 'separate national research and development, absorbing a higher proportion of total defence spending than in the US. . . We run the risk of failing to optimise scientific opportunities as they present themselves.'

Heseltine continued,

> I have spent many hours talking to my ministerial colleagues in Europe about this problem and, encouragingly, there is genuine appreciation of the cost to Europe itself of our collective inability to make more progress. There is also a general appreciation that the only way forward is political – not industrial, not military, not research-led. It is in the end only the ultimate customer, the national taxpayer, who, through their politicians, can bring about the coordinated marketplace that alone will deliver the efficiencies and economies. I do not believe that the market itself will produce such a solution. Governments must take the lead.

The starting point was to be common operational concepts and requirements, increased interdependence on research and development, and thence increasing emphasis on competition and cost-effectivenes. 'An encouraging development is the increasing tendency of industrial firms to form trans-national consortia capable of competing for large defence projects.'

Mrs Thatcher was not in Heseltine's audience at St James's Square, but she would have presided over the cabinet when it cleared the text of the 1985 defence white paper. A section is given over to 'The European Pillar'. The Western European Union (WEU) had been given new tasks in 1984. The Independent European Programme Group (IEPG) had met at full defence minister level for the first time at the end of the same year. Cooperative ventures were multiplying: the Anglo–Italian EH101 helicopter; the UK–French–German–Italian–American multi-launch rocket system; the UK–French–German anti-tank weapon Trigat; the UK–German–

Norwegian ASRAAM air-to-air missile. The European fighter aircraft (the EFA) was taking shape on the drawing boards of the United Kingdom, Germany, Italy and Spain (France had gone her own way). This was a twenty billion pound project, promising some thousand interceptor aircraft for which the agreement was signed on 2 August 1985. This grandiose project did not meet with universal approval among defence specialists. A former permanent secretary has described it as 'a classic case of changed policy without discussion and a total victory for the aerospace lobby and a total negation of Heseltine's own reorganisation'. Is the manned aircraft still the answer for the end-of-the-century battlefield? There are those experts who have their doubts.

With the appointment of Peter Levene as chief of defence equipment procurement, the ministry set its course upon a sustained drive over a period of years to bring about the necessary international cooperation.

Given the Westland Affair, which is the subject of the next chapter, it is important to quote once more from the 1985 defence white paper, the document which was the basis for the attempt by Heseltine to create a European consortium as a rival to Sikorsky. 'These are commendable achievements,' said the white paper, 'but during recent years the need for more systematic and regular cooperation has become apparent. The growing costs and technological complexity that each new generation of weapons systems needs in order to match the steady improvements in Warsaw Pact capabilities, and the relatively limited scale of national requirements among the European nations, mean that it is becoming ever more difficult to meet national requirements cost-effectively from purely national programmes...' The prose may be dense, but the message was clear enough. The white paper concluded: 'The European effort described above is not an alternative to transatlantic cooperation: on the contrary, a stronger and more cohesive European industry will contribute to the strength of the Alliance as a whole and enable Europe to cooperate more effectively on level terms with the

United States. The United Kingdom therefore intends to press ahead in this field with vigour and determination.' Both qualities were later to be much in evidence, and not simply on Heseltine's part.

A secretary of state for defence has to combine strategy with tactics. Heseltine's long-term objectives included reorganisation of the ministry, the defeat of CND, the attempt to get value for money from procurement, and the advocacy of the defence policies he had inherited. He was obliged to defend the purchase of the Trident missile as the Polaris replacement. All of this could be predicted; what cannot be is the challenge of issues which, arising quite suddenly, present problems of an acute nature. One such issue was the Ponting case.

The sinking of the Argentinian heavy cruiser, the *Belgrano*, was the most controversial incident of the Falklands War. I believe it to have been a necessary act of war, undertaken in defence of the task force at a time when its vulnerability was a cause for concern. Yet the loss of life appalled those who were opposed to the campaign to recapture the islands, and the circumstances surrounding the release of information, and the timing of the sinking, which appeared to have 'torpedoed' the Peruvian peace initiative, gave ammunition to the opponents of the government. Chief among these was Tam Dalyell.

Of all these issues, Heseltine knew nothing. He was not a member of the 'war cabinet', and very little detailed information was imparted to the cabinet itself. He was thus totally unable, upon his arrival at the ministry of defence, to defend the government's record. Since 1982 Tam Dalyell had doggedly kept asking the Prime Minister the same question: 'Why do you keep saying that HMS *Conqueror* sank the *Belgrano* immediately upon encountering it, when in fact the submarine tracked the cruiser for thirty hours before sinking it?'

Clive Ponting was head of the division responsible for advising ministers on matters to do with the Falklands War.

The initial problem with which Ponting was faced in 1984 was what advice to give Heseltine in view of a letter from Denzil Davies, the Labour Opposition's defence spokesman, which threatened to reopen the whole *Belgrano* affair. Ponting was obliged to address the question, on behalf of his political masters, of whether the government could continue to block the search for more information. Ponting did not think it could.

Heseltine's response to Ponting's opinion was sensible enough; when confronted, as he was, with a difficult political issue, he simply asked Ponting to go away and find out what really happened. Ponting then produced an account of the sinking which became known as the 'crown jewels'. (Ponting was, however, not privy to some of the most sensitive intelligence information which bore on the Royal Navy's submarine 'operations.) Having received the document, Michael then set up a group to respond to Ponting's findings. This group consisted of Sir Clive Whitmore, the permanent secretary who had been the Prime Minister's private secretary during the conflict, John Stanley, Ponting and Heseltine himself. The group operated under conditions of trust; confidences shared were not expected to be shared with other civil servants outside the group, let alone with the Opposition and general public. The possibility of a leak from so senior and important a group was naturally discounted. After several meetings, which have been described as 'pretty confused', it was decided that the secretary of state should admit to the fact that the *Belgrano* had been tracked for thirty hours prior to her sinking, but say no more because additional information, presumably to do with communications, could raise wider intelligence issues.

What Ponting revealed in two letters to Tam Dalyell was that the *Belgrano* had been steaming westwards, that is away from the 'exclusion zone', for eleven hours before it was sunk at 8 p.m. on 2 May 1982. Later it was admitted that the Prime Minister herself did not know of this until March 1984, almost two years after the events. She has said that had she known, it would not have altered her decision.

What gave cause for concern was not so much the sinking of the cruiser – the *Sun*'s vulgar headline 'Gotcha' did express the public's robust attitude towards an act of war – but the reluctance with which the government had released pertinent information, and the apparent conflict between various ministerial statements on the matter. Worse, from the government's point of view, was the credence given to the conspiracy theories of Dalyell and others, to the effect that the sinking was a political act designed to scupper the last chance of a peaceful settlement. Clive Ponting, by his breach of trust, had caused a major political scandal.

It does appear that Clive Ponting had been growing dissatisfied with his career within the civil service, and that the *Belgrano* affair gave him the chance to vent his frustrations. It is not surprising that Heseltine saw the transfer of confidential information as a blatant breach of trust, as utterly contemptible behaviour.

There were two main criticisms levelled at Michael Heseltine over his reactions to Clive Ponting's disclosures. He was accused of having sought Ponting's prosecution under Section 2 of the Official Secrets Act, and of having done so after assuring Ponting that he would not have to face charges; it was also said that Heseltine's speech in the debate in the Commons, following on Ponting's unexpected acquittal, was vindictive and unfair.

Neither of these allegations can stand. The decision to prosecute Ponting was taken, quite properly, by the law officers, and there was never any question that Heseltine could or had given Ponting any assurance about not facing charges. As to the charge of vindictiveness, one's response can only be a matter of opinion. Many people, both in politics and in the civil service, felt at the time that Ponting's behaviour was sufficiently reprehensible to justify fully Heseltine's attack upon him in the Commons.

Heseltine's anger can be explained, at least in part, from the hitherto secret documents published by the ministry of defence in time for the Commons debate. Heseltine revealed that Ponting had given ministers conflicting advice, first to withhold and then to publish information about the sinking of the cruiser. He also revealed that Ponting had written to Tam Dalyell in April 1984 urging the Labour MP to press questions about the *Belgrano* which, a few days earlier, he had advised the same ministers not to answer.

Faced with a critical Opposition motion, Heseltine replied to the effect that if the Opposition had its way, the House would be expected to support 'the constitutional novelty . . . that the most trusted civil servants, in the most secure parts of our defence establishments, should be free anonymously to draft questions for Opposition backbenchers to submit to ministers on which the selfsame leaking civil servants may then brief the ministers as to the answers they consider appropriate'.

Michael Heseltine's performance in the debate won the praise of his friends, if not of his enemies. Prior to the Westland Affair, Heseltine was no favourite of the Left. He was thought to have been ruthless in his dismissal of the Campaign for Nuclear Disarmament. What was more, the Labour Party in opposition had abandoned the Hobbesian view of the primacy of state interests with regard to matters of security, in favour of Locke. The Official Secrets Act, or more particularly Section 2, the 'catchall' section, was under attack. Governments were no longer expected to have secrets. Of the freedoms, that of information had come to assume the greatest importance. Here, or so they thought, was an arrogant man of right-wing views defending the interests of a prime minister they detested, and attempting to justify an 'atrocity', that is the sinking of the *Belgrano*. The Conservative right may have had their doubts about Michael Heseltine (and they still do), but he has never been a favourite figure on the left of British politics.

Heseltine's speech was a triumph. It was the best single parliamentary performance of the second Thatcher government. In his column in *The Times*, Geoffrey Smith wrote:

Mr Heseltine's great achievement, however, was to arouse not merely dutiful support but real enthusiasm on the Conservative benches. This success may be of consequence in Conservative politics long after the *Belgrano* has been forgotten. It might be thought that he was bound to secure a debating triumph once the decision had been taken to reveal the Ponting Memoranda. But other ministers have failed in the course of this parliament to make much of cases that were no weaker than the one Mr Heseltine deployed on Monday.

He does not have much of a personal following on the Conservative back benches. Indeed, he has been careful not to cultivate one and sometimes even gives the impression of repelling potential followers. But so many of the government's troubles over the last year or so have come from failures of presentation that his success on Monday will surely be noted by Conservative MPs.

Smith made two further points: that no minister can make progress unless he can show he can take care of himself 'in the rough exchanges of parliamentary warfare', and that Mr Ponting and Mr Dalyell had combined to give Heseltine the opportunity to show what a formidable parliamentary debater he can be.

The Ponting debate was the high water mark of Heseltine's period at defence. Those of us on the Tory back benches who took an interest in defence, wondered what next he could find to occupy himself with. In the autumn of 1985 Westland was 'a cloud no larger than a man's hand', and besides disguising his private scepticism about President Reagan's Strategic Defence Initiative, with an attempt to win research contracts for British companies, Heseltine had little to do save worry about declining resources and expanding military commitments. The more cynical observer wondered how he would be able to avoid the perils of overcommitment. The agreement to spend an additional 3% a year on defence in real terms was due to expire in the financial year 1986/7, and logic suggested yet another 'fundamental defence review' of the kind previous defence ministers had been forced to set up: a review which would lead to cuts in Britain's many commitments. John Nott had spent much of his time in office engaged in a battle with Conservative backbenchers; Heseltine had no wish to follow his predecessor's example.

Rather than do so, he would more likely have resorted to fudge. Reequipment decisions would have been postponed or abandoned, forces-in-being pared down while leaving their responsibilities intact. Fudge would have been the order of the day until the general election, after which the incoming government, and a newly appointed secretary of state, would no longer be able to procrastinate.

Fudge has indeed been George Younger's chosen course. The Trident programme has continued to absorb a large proportion of the equipment budget; the British Army of the Rhine has received fewer of its new Challenger tanks, and the numbers of Tornado aircraft coming into service have been cut. Old battles such as the one against the Campaign for Nuclear Disarmament and Labour's anti-nuclear defence policy, have had to be refought.

During all this time Heseltine would have been excluded from the politics of economics, his voice in the battle between 'wets' and 'dries', radicals and consolidators, heard only behind closed cabinet doors. If Mrs Thatcher had sent him to defence nearly three years before to get him out of the way, she was in no hurry to bring him back into the centre of affairs. Had not the Westland crisis broken, Heseltine would have had little to which to look forward, save more of the same. He was a minister who had tasted success. He was becoming increasingly frustrated, bored with his lot. The charge of his discontents had been laid; all that was missing was the fuse.

Over the Top

The fuse was to be Heseltine's growing impatience with the Prime Minister. The spark was Westland. He had grown steadily more disillusioned with the style in which Mrs Thatcher conducted her cabinet and government. Heseltine is a sensitive political operator who seeks harmony. Not for him the urge to dominate and to instruct. He found Mrs Thatcher's way of dealing with her colleagues wearying. Heseltine's method of working had always been to give others their heads and permit them their opinions; Mrs Thatcher, on the other hand, loves nothing better than to lead from the front. She is not a good listener. Not for her the 'collecting of voices'.

Heseltine had not often crossed swords with her, as the ministry of defence was, ironically enough, isolated in part from her attentions. But he had been a spectator at the humiliations of others. On one occasion Heseltine had threatened res' nation, thereby forcing a change of mind upon Mrs Thatcher and the cabinet, over the order for new frigates from Cammell Laird in Birkenhead. Michael had not forgotten his 'viceroyalty' of Liverpool. It was to be a hard-won victory, for the memory of her defeat lingered in the Prime Minister's mind as the Westland crisis rose to its peak. A member of the cabinet told me months after Heseltine's resignation, that he believed the blame for the whole 'affair' was Margaret's. 'She failed to manage Heseltine properly. She is no good at man-management.'

Had Heseltine sat alone one evening in November 1985 in a better restaurant than Long John Silver's, with the back of a larger envelope on which to draw up a balance sheet, what would he have jotted down? As a first heading on the debit side he might have written 'The fun has gone out of politics'.

He was probably the best-known minister in Mrs Thatcher's administration. Geoffrey Howe was respected but dull. Nigel Lawson politically controversial and unloved. Peter Walker had enjoyed a good miners' strike but was isolated within the cabinet and the parliamentary party. Norman Fowler was an apparatchik. Norman Tebbit had been winged by misfortune, and Keith Joseph was a burnt-out case. Only Kenneth Baker's star was in the ascendant. Mrs Thatcher's own position was more vulnerable than the leader writers of our largely foreign-owned newspapers were willing to admit. Imperious and unpopular in the country, she was sustained by her party's instinct for self-preservation, the inertia of her backbenchers, and the absence of an obvious successor. Opposition to her and her policies was expressed openly by relatively small groups of her party, such as Francis Pym's Centre Forward within Westminster, and the Tory Reform Group and the Young Conservatives without.

He might also have noted (over a glass of unremarkable wine, for Heseltine is abstemious, eating and drinking little), that, despite his fame, he had no personal following. There were but a handful of the devoted. But there were many others who remained suspicious of a man they professed not to know. One minister of state, politically far to the right of Michael, describes Heseltine as 'bogus'. He likens him to a well-known West End jeweller's where the amorous used to buy deceptively attractive jewels to reward their lovers. 'All his goods in the shop window.' Heseltine has always attracted hostility both from the Thatcherites, who are, more often than not, petit bourgeois, and from the gents, who see him as an 'arriviste'.

In 1980 Heseltine allowed himself to be proposed and seconded for membership of Pratt's, a foolish move. The candidate's book became a battleground, and the then plain William Whitelaw was heard trumpeting his disapproval. At that, Peter Hillmore of the *Observer* got hold of the story. The Duke of Devonshire, who owns the club, intervened, and ordered that the election process be restarted. Heseltine was eventually admitted into the smartest of London clubs, but he makes little or no use of it.

In public life one is either flattered or abused. Heseltine had turned fifty, made a million, and was a public figure of the sort that can go nowhere unrecognised. He had demonstrated his oratorical skills both on the political platform and in parliament. He had reorganised a great ministry. Kept at arm's length by the Prime Minister, Heseltine was bored. What should he do next?

Stories about Heseltine were the common currency of Commons gossip. The occasion at which Heseltine had been introduced by a scarlet master of ceremonies at a City dinner following with this splendid build-up – 'My Lord Mayor, my lords, ladies and gentlemen, pray silence for the secretary of state for defence, Mr Michael Bentine' – was widely relished. In October 1985, in the lull before the Westland storm, I shared a table in the Members' Dining-Room with Heseltine. His patronage was infrequent, but just how rare was brought home to us both when, after giving his order to the waitress, she asked him for his name. This, too, gave rise to merriment. Three months later not even a Commons' waitress would have been in any doubt.

I do not intend to retell in any detail the story of Westland. Readers who seek a definitive account of this tortuous and complicated affair should read *Not With Honour* by Messrs Linklater and Leigh, published by the *Observer* with Sphere Books in 1986. What I do intend to do is to examine the affair as a privileged spectator at some of the events, and to do so in a way which will, hopefully, throw light upon Michael Heseltine's motives and actions.

A list of the dramatis personae of this strange three-act drama would include the following:

The Prime Minister: imperious, indecisive and belligerent. 'Who shall rid me of this turbulent priest?' Over the leak of selected parts of the Mayhew letter, she willed the ends; the responsibility for the means employed is hers.

Lord Whitelaw, Margaret's deputy: loyal to Mrs Thatcher and a sworn enemy of Heseltine's. He harbours an aristocratic contempt for 'new money'. Had Whitelaw John Mortimer's skill with a pen, Heseltine would have been his model for Leslie Titmuss.

Leon Brittan, secretary of state for trade and industry: a clever lawyer with little or no following among simpler Tory MPs. Took on Heseltine over the future of Westland as the company's 'sponsoring minister'. Confessed to having misled the House over the Lygo letter, and resigned. Greater love hath no man than to lay down his life for his Leader. The fall guy.

Sir Patrick Mayhew, the solicitor general. An Oxford contemporary and friend of Heseltine's. A bluff and competent lawyer. Of all the characters in the Westland Affair, the one with the most to complain about. Used improperly and without his knowledge in an attempt to do down Heseltine.

Sir John Cuckney, chairman of Westland. Like Michael Heseltine, an Old Salopian, though they have nothing else in common. A rescuer of companies in distress, he was appointed at the behest of the Bank of England and his appointment came as a relief to the company's bankers, Barclays and NatWest, who were supporting it with massive overdrafts. Cuckney had the additional task of retaining the banks' confidence. Close to the Prime Minister both in temperament and objective. A tough and uncompromising customer.

John Wakeham, the government chief whip. The keeper of the party's interest. Worked first to keep Heseltine within the government, but grew increasingly anxious about the political consequences of so violent and public a disagreement. Helped to concoct Mrs Thatcher's ultimatum which she delivered at the cabinet meeting on 9 January 1986. Shrewd, mild in manner, his contribution to keeping the ship afloat with two men overboard and the Captain confined to her cabin was decisive.

Sir Humphrey Atkins: at the time chairman of the Defence Select Committee of the Commons which later conducted two enquiries into the affair. A good-looking lightweight who left the hard questions to Michael Mates MP and Dr John Gilbert.

Sir Robert Armstrong: the cabinet secretary and head of the civil service. He carried out the enquiry into the circumstances surrounding the Mayhew leak on the orders of Sir Michael Havers, the attorney general. Gave evidence on the part of other civil servants before the select committee. Later in the year visited Australia but on different business.

And a cast of hundreds, including the leader of the Opposition, Neil Kinnock, who in debate let an opportunity slip; David Steel who accused the Prime Minister of 'wasting police time', and Dr David Owen who asked all the right questions; Sir Austin Pearce of British Aerospace; Sir Raymond Lygo, a crusty admiral who sailed to the aid of the European consortium and torpedoed Leon Brittan. There were three choruses: the corps of political correspondents who wrote ceaselessly; the members of the Tory Party's 1922 Committee who, while relishing every moment of an unfolding drama, did their best to keep their faces straight; and the general public which, while not understanding a great deal of what was taking place, did not much approve of what they did understand. Sir John Hoskyns played no part in the affair, but his dictum that 'the Tory never panics save in times of crisis' once, before Westland, made the Prime Minister laugh.

In early spring 1985 Westland, a public company which manufactured helicopters in Yeovil, Somerset, began to show signs of impending financial crisis; bankruptcy threatened. As far as the ministry of defence was concerned, this was a cloud no bigger than a man's hand. By that autumn, however, the ministry was obliged to concern itself with the company's affairs, and Heseltine's attention was drawn to the necessity of finding a solution.

It should first be said that there are those who believe that had Heseltine done his homework back in the spring of 1985, most of the problem could have been diverted. The conventional view of Heseltine's advisors at the ministry of defence is that Westland first became apparent as a major problem in October 1985. Sir Frank Cooper believes that is rubbish; and that it was 'as plain as a pikestaff' that Westland would present Heseltine with major difficulties as far back as February 1985. During that summer Heseltine had been in no hurry to come to the rescue of 'a bankrupt company' in whose management he had no confidence; had he begun his initiative to find a European solution earlier than he did, the course of history . . .

His dilatoriness was all the more surprising, given the passion he brought to the European cause. He most certainly did not belatedly espouse the principle of European cooperation in any opportunistic sense. As we have seen, Heseltine has a long history of support for Europe which can be traced back to his years as a junior minister in Edward Heath's government. As secretary of state, he had concentrated his attention upon the problem of European arms procurement, and had spent much of 1984 working towards an agreement to manufacture the European fighter aircraft – an exercise during which he had greatly impressed his opposite numbers in Germany and France with his sense of commitment. If Westland, a relatively small and thus only marginally important company, was not afforded the attention it was eventually to demand, the blame should be shared between Heseltine and Sir Clive Whitmore.

When we ask, therefore, why Heseltine should have put his career in such jeopardy over this issue, why he was prepared to clash so violently with the Prime Minister, part of the answer can be found in the genuine fervour of his belief in Europe and European cooperation which was strongly at variance with Mrs Thatcher's agnosticism. To a politician of Heseltine's view, temperament and age, support for the European cause is a fundamental political belief; the Prime Minister, on the other hand, has never been enamoured of foreigners, save perhaps for right-wing Americans. On the subject of European unity, she is at best a Gaullist, at worst a secret sympathiser of the likes of Teddy Taylor, Enoch Powell and Edward du Cann, whose hostility to the concept is undisguised. Her demands at the Dublin 'summit' of 1979 for 'our money back' gave grave offence to the party's pro-European idealists.

That Michael was driven by ardent commitment can be demonstrated by Sir Patrick Mayhew's remark to me at the height of the Westland Affair. Paddy stopped me in the 'aye' lobby and reminded me of the passionate intensity with which, thirty years before, Heseltine had fought the 'Battle of the OUCA Elections' – whether or not the committee of the Oxford Conservatives, or the membership as a whole, should elect the officers of the association. 'Just like Westland,' was the view of the solicitor general.

The other reason for Heseltine's head-on collision with the Prime Minister was his dislike of her and all her works. The word he used, in private, to describe her economic policies, was 'lunatic'. Moreover, he felt her to be unpleasant to work with and a bit of a bully. Perhaps had he resorted to coded public attacks in the style of many of his cabinet colleagues, past and present, he would have been able to blow off steam. But, as we have seen, his public stance was one of uncritical loyalty. He never failed to behave with circumspection in the 'war' between wets and dries. Heseltine may not have been 'one of us', as defined by Margaret Thatcher, but he had certainly not taken up arms with the likes of Francis Pym, Jim

Prior and Ian Gilmour. His hostility was private, but deep-seated.

Heseltine had little love for Leon Brittan either. He saw Brittan taking an opportunity over the battle of Westland to make some political capital and restore his fortunes. Heseltine took aim at the bigger of the two birds; he was obliged to take what satisfaction he could from bringing down the smaller. The irony of the whole affair lay in Heseltine's failure to enlist the support of his colleagues, Brittan's abandonment by his leader and rejection by his colleagues on the back benches, and the survival of the prime minister who was herself widely disliked. John Wakeham issued an order of the day which contained the trite if effective message that it was time for all good men to come to the aid of the party. We did.

Boredom may well have been yet another reason for Heseltine's precipitation. He had held the office of defence secretary for almost three years, a period during which he had been actively engaged on many different activities, including a major reorganisation of the structure of the ministry. He had played a large part in winning the election. He had had also to be content with the role of spectator of events. Mrs Thatcher, it was true, left him largely to his own devices, a departure for which he was grateful. He was, on the other hand, excluded from those cabinet committees the task of which was to lubricate the 'Thatcher revolution'. Heseltine had long coveted the department of trade and industry, the recently acquired fief of Leon Brittan, whose loyalty to the Prime Minister and to her policies was beyond reproach. It is often asserted by commentators that ministers are too swiftly shifted; the truth is that ambitious and powerful personalities can be kept in place too long.

Heseltine was not unaware of his growing reputation. Field Marshal 'Dwin' Bramall has said that he sees several similarities between Heseltine and Churchill. They share, says the former chief of the defence staff, the same vision and 'the ability to move mountains'. Heseltine, like Churchill, is clever, a good speaker and 'has a high opinion of his abilities'.

Bramall does not stop there. Like Churchill, Heseltine is 'not good with people'. He is, in fact, 'self-centred, inconsiderate, so bad in the way he treats colleagues and staff'. Here, we hear echoes of the reorganisation. Heseltine has, like Churchill, enormous energy and a great ability 'to put things together'. When charged by the field marshal with 'treating people like part of the furniture', Heseltine (says Bramall) 'would always make his excuses with a certain refreshing, boyish, candid charm'. The hearts of grizzled soldiers evidently melt at a lower temperature than those of prime ministers. The comparison with Churchill can only be carried so far; Heseltine does not smoke and scarcely drinks. And he is addicted to knocking down walls.

'Dwin' Bramall claims that Heseltine is a 'fundamentally political animal'. In his view, many defence ministers see the split between defence and politics as being fifty/fifty. Heseltine's perception was, according to Bramall, seventy-five in favour of politics, twenty-five in favour of defence. In which case, it is curious that Heseltine did not spot the political implications of the failure of the Westland Company more quickly than he did.

Bramall retired at the end of November 1985. It is his view that it was only when Heseltine saw the Sikorsky deal with Westland taking shape that he realised such an arrangement with an American company would not fit into his plans for future European collaboration. The field marshal also feels that Heseltine saw an opportunity for taking on the Prime Minister over the issue of collective cabinet responsibility, and winning.

The Westland Affair was about helicopters. MPs are not interested in helicopters, still less in the problems of European arms procurement. Defence is not a major interest. Events such as the upsurge of the Campaign for Nuclear Disarmament, or the cancellation of a major weapon such as Skybolt in 1962, can conscript the interest of MPs. Most of the time, however, defence remains an esoteric subject, the province of a diminishing number of ex-service officers like Major Sir Patrick Wall, a handful of former ministers, like Sir Antony Buck and Keith Speed, and a few strategy buffs like John Wilkinson, Cyril Townsend and Michael Mates. Winston Churchill shared a family interest in the concern.

Among those who took an interest in defence – and the weekly meetings of the Tory Party's Defence Committee rarely attract more than a dozen MPs, summoned more often than not to listen to some manufacturer with something to sell – helicopters were a good deal less of a draw than Trident missiles and their submarines. The same might well have applied within the ministry of defence.

The procurement of helicopters was the sort of problem for which the enlarged central policy review staff was surely designed. Previously helicopters, like the Royal Marines and the Parachute Regiment, had fallen into a crevasse between the three services. The rapid movement of troops by helicopter on the battlefield is the responsibility of the Royal Air Force. Troop-carrying helicopters are flown by RAF pilots, and procured by the RAF budget. This budget was considered generous by the other two services for the RAF spends almost as much on equipment as the Army and Navy put together. There has been a discreet elation, in recent years, in the higher reaches of the Air Force at having been allotted no less than five major types of fixed-wing aircraft. And this at a time when the role of the manned aircraft in the missile age was coming under scrutiny. Among airmen, ferrying the army by helicopter seemed to enjoy a low priority.

At the beginning of 1985 even the Royal Air Force budget was feeling the pinch. The cost of 185 Tornadoes was higher than had been expected. This did not prevent the Royal Air Force from pressing vigorously for the new European fighter aircraft, but it did mean that there were no obvious funds to place the order which could have saved Britain's only major helicopter company.

Westland is not a very large company. Traditionally some

60% of its turnover arose from the Yeovil helicopter factory. In 1985 the world market for helicopters was depressed. In 1977 when British Aerospace was formed, Westland was not included. Without orders from the ministry of defence the company could not hope to survive, let alone flourish. Despite pleas by Mrs Thatcher and others to the effect that things should be left to the market, this central fact in the Westland saga seems to have eluded many. A defence industry is not like any other; the denial of a government contract is not just a pity, it precludes all possibility of exports. Foreigners ask why they should buy British-made defence equipment if the British themselves are not prepared to do so.

The failure of the W30, the Westland project for a civil commuter helicopter, brought matters to a head. If there had been such a thing as a helicopter commuter market, Westland would have made a killing, for there would have been no competition. Sadly, there was no such market. Worst of all, the Westland board had no experience of the commercial market. The company had lived a sheltered life, depending on regular infusions of money from the ministry of defence.

Their competitors abroad were mainly much larger companies, all of them sustained by government purchasing. Within Europe, for example, Aérospatiale (France) and Agusta (Italy) are state-controlled. American companies like Sikorsky can confidently count on a regular slice of a defence budget over ten times the size of that of the United Kingdom. The size of the United States market enabled Sikorsky to cut costs and increase production to the point at which they were producing twice as many helicopters as the whole of Europe with little over half the manpower.

As we have seen, there are those who assert that Heseltine should have anticipated the crisis. In October 1984 he had been warned by the then chairman, Lord Aldington, that Westland would be in serious trouble if funds were not forthcoming from the ministry of defence to develop a helicopter for the Air Force. At the same time John Wilkinson MP warned that urgent action must be taken to save the company. There was no doubt a case for Heseltine to adopt then and there the solution for which he was later to fight so strenuously: a European consortium. British governments were committed by the 1978 Declaration of Principles agreed with France, Germany and Italy, to develop 'families' of helicopters, including naval attack, army attack, and army transport vehicles. Heseltine had two reasons for not acting: firstly, none of the services wanted a helicopter. The Navy had the Sea King and was looking forward to getting the EH101. The Royal Air Force had no money, while the Army could not make up its mind. In fact, it was not until the autumn of 1986 that the central policy staff came to a decision. In March 1985 Heseltine announced that the Air Staff Target 404, for which Westland had hoped that the W30 would win the contract, had been withdrawn.

Secondly, the secretary of state had no confidence in Westland's management. He was not alone in his view. It was echoed in the department of trade and industry. What was even more significant was the corroboration of this view of Westland which came from Bill Paul of Sikorsky who accused the Somerset firm of 'living in an ivory tower'. Paul felt he could not do business with Westland as constituted. Heseltine had already cancelled a helicopter maintenance contract and put it out to tender. It was won by Alan Bristow the millionaire helicopter entrepreneur. Heseltine had not got on well with Toby Aldington, and Aldington's successor as chairman, Sir Basil Blackwell, did not win the secretary of state's confidence either. In this climate, it is hardly surprising that Heseltine had no time for Westland, and was ready to wash his hands of the company.

Westland had been kept going by *tranches* of public money. Launch aid of forty million pounds had been swallowed up by the W30 project, and there was even some uncertainty as to whether the money would ever be returned, or even if Westland would be compelled to match it from their own resources. Heseltine is, as we have seen, an interventionist, ready to subsidise deserving cases. Mrs

Thatcher is not, although she is prepared to subsidise exports, as was seen in her unsuccessful attempt to persuade the Indians to buy the W30. Three choices were looming: to go on as before with more government money; to sell the company off, presumably to Sikorsky, thus freeing the British taxpayer from some, at least, of the demands likely to be made upon it, but at the price of American dominance of the helicopter market; and a trans-European solution, which would call in aid from the contributions of the French, German and Italian taxpayer besides our own.

It looked for a while as if Alan Bristow, a former test pilot and ex-Westland employee, might come riding to the rescue, although there was no love lost between him and Westland. He had the idea of rescuing the company provided the W30 were scrapped and links were formed with Sikorsky. Heseltine was, for a time, inclined to smile upon this solution. In May 1985 Blackwell invited Sikorsky to make a bid for his company. But the Americans were not prepared to invest in the old régime. In June Blackwell recommended the shareholders to accept Bristow's proposal. Bristow himself, however, was now having second thoughts. He had discovered that he might be obliged to repay the government the forty million pounds launch money. He went further and told the government that without more money Westland would be unable to build the EH101 for the Royal Navy. Heseltine offered to write off half the launch money if the DTI would write off the other twenty million pounds.

It is thus unfair to accuse Heseltine of neglecting the issue. Had Mrs Thatcher permitted Norman Tebbit at the department of trade and industry to put his hand in his pocket, there would have been no Westland Affair. But it is not unreasonable to assert that Heseltine did not appreciate the political implications of giving Sikorsky a foot in the door until it was too late.

American enterprises are not in the habit of rescuing moribund foreign companies for altruistic motives. Sikorsky was desperate to sell its Black Hawk helicopter into Europe.

Heseltine, having reorganised the ministry of defence itself, had devoted his energies towards European collaboration. He could point to the agreement to build the European fighter aircraft. By the autumn of 1985 Heseltine had come to realise that the whole basis of the 1978 agreement could be called into question, were so large a company as Sikorsky, and one so highly protected within the US, to mount a challenge. The cuckoo was about to lay its egg.

At the end of June 1985 Blackwell was replaced as chairman by Sir John Cuckney. From the beginning Heseltine stressed to Cuckney that it was not his, Heseltine's, job to save Westland. That responsibility lay, if anywhere, with the department of trade and industry. This was the case, although it does mask an anomaly which surely deserves attention. No major defence contractor can survive in Britain without regular orders from the ministry of defence. But the task of the ministry is the defence of the realm, not the resolution of Britain's industrial problems. The ministry of defence has long recognised that it may well have to dip into its pocket to help out, but it is not the role of its secretary of state to give the kiss of life to the ailing.

In September Bill Paul asked Heseltine whether he would buy the Black Hawk. Heseltine replied that he had neither the funds for it, nor the operational requirement. The former was certainly true. Heseltine had, on 2 August, signed the European fighter aircraft agreement committing Britain to an international project involving twenty billion pounds. Now, for the first time, as he later told the House of Commons Industry Select Committee, he recognised the threat posed by Sikorsky. 'Sikorsky were going to use every device known to man to get the British government to buy Black Hawk. . . They were deeply embarrassed at how unsuccessful it had been, how few they had sold. They had tried all over the place.'

At about this time Norman Tebbit was moved sideways to become chairman of the Conservative Party and paymaster general. His place at the department of trade and industry was taken by Leon Brittan, who had been none too happy at the home office. His eager anticipation of Mrs Thatcher's expected disapproval of the BBC TV programme 'Real Lives', caused him to rebuke the corporation for a programme he had not, in fact, seen. Leon Brittan, as events were soon to show, was never slow at doing what he believed to be the Prime Minister's bidding.

As a lawyer, Leon Brittan specialised in defamation. A former chairman of the Bow Group, he had long sought a safe seat in parliament, but his progress, when he finally arrived, was spectacularly swift. He is of Lithuanian origin and the brother of the celebrated journalist and monetarist guru, Sam Brittan. Leon's parliamentary ascent had been a shade too steep for his more pedestrian colleagues. He was popularly regarded by the tea-room brutes as a 'creep' whose love for the Prime Minister had not gone unrewarded. His appointment at trade and industry confirmed the melancholy fact that the expertise within the Tory Party lies not in industry but in finance.

Heseltine and Brittan had worked harmoniously in the past when Brittan had been chief secretary to the treasury. The commitment to honour the 3% annual increase in real terms in defence spending had helped to smooth away any disagreement between the treasury and a high-spending departmental minister. The two men met twice in October 1985 to discuss Westland. Heseltine outlined proposals for a European solution, and Brittan offered no objection. As neither of them favoured bailing out the company, the only practical alternative to Sikorsky had to be Europe. Brittan has since claimed that his attitude (interpreted by Heseltine as a 'green light') was coloured by the probability that the Sikorsky option would involve the government in further payments, but it is hard to imagine how he could suppose that the European alternative would not.

Heseltine now set to work mobilising what his opponents were to call his 'stage army'. Meetings were held between Agusta, MB&M, and Aérospatiale. Sir John Cuckney found the whole European alternative hard to believe; why should anybody want to come to Westland's rescue unless they had the motives of Sikorsky? At best the European alternative might conceivably improve Sikorsky's bid. In November 1985 Heseltine exploited his close relations with his European opposite numbers to invest his rival solution with a remarkable credibility. He held a convention of European national armaments directors, the top officials in each national ministry of defence responsible for European collaboration. They agreed in principle on a third European helicopter project alongside the EH101 and the NH90. Heseltine undertook to place an order for it.

Sir John Cuckney became alarmed, and believing that what Heseltine was doing was at variance with government policy, went over his head to Mrs Thatcher. The Prime Minister, who had paid scant attention to the problems of Westland, needed little encouragement from Cuckney; Heseltine stood accused of insubordination. Cuckney argued that the European *démarche* might scare off Sikorsky, thus stampeding Barclays and NatWest. And the impending end-of-year deadline was enough to induce a mixture of alarm and outrage at Number 10. Westland's accounts were due to be published early in December, showing losses of up to one hundred million. Not only the two joint stock banks but parliament itself would want to know the reason why.

There began a series of meetings between ministers. Two such were held on 5 and 6 December. Both have been described as 'bad tempered'. It seems that Heseltine found himself in a minority of one, but he persisted in his argument that it would be discourteous to our European partners were the government to reject their proposal out of hand. With some reluctance, the Prime Minister referred the matter to a meeting of the Economic Subcommittee of the cabinet (EA) to be held on the following Monday.

The EA meeting on 9 December was one of the liveliest of Mrs Thatcher's premiership. Besides those ministers who had met twice in the previous week (Tebbit, MacGregor, Heseltine, Whitelaw, Howe, Biffen and Brittan), there were present Kenneth Clarke, on behalf of Lord Young, Peter Walker, Michael Spicer for Nicholas Ridley, Kenneth Baker, and the chief of the party's 'secret police', the chief whip, John Wakeham. Sir John Cuckney was also invited to take part.

Cuckney told the meeting that he could only consider the European consortium alternative if it were to be 'fully underwritten' by the British government. This rubbing together of fingers alarmed many and appalled those who were reluctant to spend government money. Heseltine countered by asking for time; time for the consortium to submit a proper proposal. It would do so, Heseltine argued, by the end of the week. Until then the recommendation of the national armaments directors should stand. Heseltine was later to claim that the majority of the meeting sided with him. After two hours of heated argument, not least between Heseltine and Brittan, and Heseltine and Mrs Thatcher, the Prime Minister, according to one account, 'slammed the table in front of her and said, "Very well, we'll have to meet again on Friday at four o'clock, after the stock exchange has closed." '

We shall never know what really happened. Whatever the truth of the matter, the undertaking proved to be the turning point of the whole Westland affair. Mrs Thatcher has no doubts:

'The conclusions of the cabinet Economic Committee on 9 December laid down a clear policy, and that made a further meeting unnecessary. No decision to hold a further meeting was taken or recorded. No meeting had been agreed so there was nothing to cancel.'

Heseltine, for his part, has no doubts:

'We know that it was the Prime Minister who said there would be a meeting on the Friday and we know it was the Prime Minister who cancelled the meeting. So there is no doubt who is responsible for the decision.'

Whatever the Prime Minister may or may not have wanted, there is no doubt that calls were made from the cabinet office fixing arrangements for a further meeting. Nicholas Ridley is

believed to have noted it, as did Lord Young. Friday afternoon is a bad time for ministers and MPs, all of whom want
either to go home or to visit their constituencies. The
prospect of a meeting then would not have been welcome.

Linklater and Leigh in their definitive account of the affair,
claim that the 'meeting' was cancelled on the Wednesday
morning on instructions from Downing Street. The misunderstanding, if that is what it was, could be explained in
one of two ways. Either the error was noted within the
cabinet office or the department of trade and industry tipped
off Number 10 as to the grave implications of holding such a
meeting. Heseltine seemed to have persuaded a majority to
his way of thinking on the Monday; was there not a risk of
his carrying Friday as well?

The effect on Michael Heseltine of the 'meeting that never
was' was little short of traumatic. He had been playing for
high stakes and it appeared that a simple change of rules had
scuppered his chances. Mrs Thatcher is nothing if not a
ruthless operator in the pursuit of what she sees to be her
interest. Heseltine risked losing credibility with the Euro-
peans, many of whom believed that his initiative was already
government policy. When he learnt of the cancellation of the
Friday meeting from Richard Mottram, his private secretary
at the ministry, Heseltine was, in his own words, 'absolutely
shattered'.

Should he have been? He had, after all, been mounting a
direct challenge to the Prime Minister and to her policies.
And politics is a rough trade. The cliché that 'there is no love
at the top' was truer for the two Thatcher administrations
than for many others. It was not simply a matter of Mrs
Thatcher's personality, which, it has been said, 'combines
self-righteousness with a strange lack of self-confidence'. Mrs
Thatcher is, as she never tires of telling, a 'conviction
politician'. She was once a simple rightwinger, and was, as
such, an object of some suspicion among her more moderate colleagues. James Prior tells it in his autobiography
A Balance of Power that he and others wished to exclude her

from the shadow cabinet of the late 'sixties on the grounds that, although much the most able of the available women MPs, she was of the sort that would prove difficult to 'get rid of'. Prior always was a master of the understatement. Love her or loathe her, and few are neutral, no one can doubt her sticking power.

Mrs Thatcher was, however, more than a strong-willed woman. She was also fighting a battle of her own. Having acquired in the late 'seventies, when leader of the Opposition, a credo of her own, 'something borrowed, something blue' ('borrowed' from Professor Milton Friedman), she was determined to have her way with her cabinets, despite the uncomfortable fact that she was often in a minority. But the power of the Prime Minister is very great. Not only can she hire and fire, but she determines the composition of the numerous cabinet subcommittees where the important decisions are, in fact, taken. She also controls the cabinet agenda. Under Mrs Thatcher, the tendency which was already apparent, towards greater Prime Ministerial control of the cabinet, has been magnified. The dictates of her personality and the demands of her policies have made her very much the prima donna *inter pares*.

She did not like Heseltine. Mrs Thatcher requires devotion as well as obedience, neither of which did she get from Michael Heseltine. Never 'one of us', he had been sent to the ministry of defence to get him out of her way. Now he had returned with a challenge to her more formidable than any she had experienced.

As I have said, Mrs Thatcher is simply not Michael's type. He found Mrs Thatcher, sweet and sour, to be not to his taste. Her Conservatism was most certainly not his, and he disapproved strongly of her imperiousness, of her way, on occasion, of dealing with cabinet colleagues. She had now, or so he believed, gone back on her word – but this tactic could hardly have come as a complete surprise. After the meeting that never was, Heseltine began to talk about resignation for the first time. Not surprisingly, the advice he got from his friends was to stay put and fight his corner. Sadly Heseltine had not enough friends.

Mrs Thatcher told the Commons a month later that no meeting had been 'formally fixed' and therefore there could be no question of it being cancelled. It was, in fact, in the course of being formally fixed when the arrangements were countermanded on the Wednesday morning. It had therefore not been formally fixed, any more than it had been decided to hold it to the accompaniment of light music. It had not been fixed; but Heseltine and others were to insist that it had been 'arranged'.

Would it have been wiser for the Prime Minister to have followed her instinct, and to have held the meeting on that Friday? I think Heseltine, had he failed to carry his point at a second meeting, would have been prepared to abide by the decision. Would Mrs Thatcher have been prepared to acquiesce in her defeat had he succeeded? The most probable outcome of the meeting that never was would have been a compromise that would have permitted Heseltine a period of grace. Had that been the case, there might have been no cause to make use of the solicitor general's letter without his knowledge or permission. It was, of course, the Mayhew leak which so gravely damaged Mrs Thatcher's reputation.

Michael Heseltine may privately have considered resignation, but he fought on. Mrs Thatcher, with the row between them public knowledge, must have given thought to ridding herself of her secretary of state. Later, she was to say on television that had she done so, the public would have said 'bossy boots'. But, in the meantime, she held a council of war. On Wednesday 18 December Sir Robert Armstrong, Lord Whitelaw, John Wakeham and Bernard Ingham met at Downing Street in order to draft a letter to Heseltine that would lay down conditions as to his conduct over the Affair. It was a meeting of heavyweights: Armstrong, fresh from a dispute with Heseltine over the cabinet minutes; Whitelaw who cannot abide him; Wakeham, who was fearful for the government's reputation, and Ingham who had carried Mrs

Thatcher's banner in a hundred battles. In the event, it was Ingham who cou selled caution, not wishing to precipitate Heseltine's resignation. No such letter was sent.

Over the next three weeks battle was joined. Openly partisan, Heseltine drew the attention of his friends to an episode in 'Spitting Image' when the Prime Minister, in cabinet, is served a piece of steak. 'What about the vegetables?' she is asked. 'They'll have the same as me,' is her reply. Heseltine was, he assured his friends, no Brussels sprout. Nor was he. He had already mobilised the support of four European ministers of defence, the industrial commissioner of the Community, British Aerospace, GEC, of which James Prior had become chairman, and much editorial support. Mrs Thatcher's watchword was neutrality; the battle was to be fought between Heseltine and Brittan, with the latter coming off much the worst. Brittan was no match for Heseltine in the open; behind the scenes he was to prove to be too clever for his own good.

At the cabinet meeting on 18 December the Prime Minister had declared that ministers should avoid making public comments on Westland. Heseltine agreed, but reserved the right to respond to questions on the subject.

Then began the episode of the three letters. Heseltine made a statement to the effect that were Westland to go Sikorsky's way, it would, as far as the ministry of defence was concerned, face a bleak future. The Black Hawk would not be purchased, and the company would be excluded from all joint projects within Europe. Heseltine followed up this bombshell by attempting to set up a meeting with Sir John Cuckney.

Michael took it into his head that if only he could meet his opponent face to face, he could persuade Cuckney to agree to the kind of solution he, Heseltine, sought. A few days before Christmas, therefore, he rang to propose that he drive down to Cuckney's house in Kent with a team of advisors to cut through the arguments and sign a 'heads of agreement' document there and then. Had the meeting taken place, it is

149

not known what Heseltine would have offered Cuckney, but in all probability it would have been German sales for Westland.

But Cuckney was under strain, his wife was ill; he was looking forward to a quiet Christmas. Heseltine's somewhat theatrical gesture – presumably motivated by his view that there are times when you have to talk tough to these City people – served only to offend him deeply, and to galvanise him into launching a counterattack. He was already working closely with the Prime Minister, who had told him that there would be no more ministerial campaigning.

In order to elicit a response from Downing Street which he could use to his advantage, the chairman of Westland wrote to the Prime Minister as follows:

> . . .It would greatly help my board to know if Westland would no longer be considered a European company by the government, if a minority shareholding were to be acquired by a major international group from a NATO country outside Europe.
>
> The question is of fundamental importance in view of the statement. . .from the ministry of defence that only by joining the so-called European Consortium would Westland be in a position to take responsibility for the British share of European helicopter collaborative projects. . .

As if by lightning, a previously drafted reply was sent from Downing Street to Leon Brittan with a memo to the effect that the final letter had to be checked by the law officers. The draft which was returned to Mrs Thatcher at 4 p.m. on New Year's Eve said exactly what Cuckney could have wished.

> As long as Westland continues to carry on business in the UK, the government will, of course, regard it as a British and therefore a European company, and will support it in pursuing British interests in Europe.
>
> Government policy will remain that Britain should procure its helicopters from the most cost-effective source.

Against this background, the government would wish to
see Westland play a full part in existing and future
European collaborative projects. . .

A copy of this draft, apparently originating from the DTI,
reached Heseltine later that afternoon. Smoke was supposed
to have issued from Heseltine. Under pressure, he responded
by ordering his officials to draft an extra section on to the
letter, repeating the ministry of defence's position, i.e., that in
the event of a deal with Sikorsky, Britain would not buy the
Black Hawk and European governments would probably
refuse to cooperate with Westland. Having done this, Heseltine asked the solicitor general to come and see him straight
away.

The result was what Heseltine wanted. After scrutinising
the draft, Mayhew told the DTI that it might contain
'material inaccuracies'. After much toing and froing between
Mayhew and Downing Street, it was necessary for Mrs
Thatcher to add yet another paragraph to the letter. This
read:

Some of these [European projects] are still at a very early
stage and all of them require the agreement of the companies and governments – including HMG – concerned. In
this connection you should be aware of indications from
European governments and companies that they currently
take the view that a number of projects in which Westland
are expecting to participate in cooperation with other
European companies may be lost to Westland if the United
Technologies (Sikorsky)/Fiat proposals are accepted.

Richard Mottram, Heseltine's private secretary, ran his master to earth later that night in a Fleet Street restaurant. Mrs
Thatcher proposed to tack on yet another paragraph to the
rapidly lengthening letter. It read:

I can assure you that whichever of the two proposals
currently under consideration the company chooses to
accept, the government would continue to support West-

land's wish to participate in these projects, and would resist to the best of its ability attempts by others to discriminate against Westland.

Fifteen all?

At about this time, with two cabinet ministers in open conflict, Sir Clive Whitmore paid a call upon Sir Robert Armstrong to seek reassurance. The partisanship into which Whitmore had been drawn by his secretary of state was highly unusual. Was it also improper? Armstrong who was, at the beginning of 1986, still unknown to the public at large, felt that Whitmore was behaving quite correctly.

The affair of the second letter followed two days later. Heseltine rang David Horne of the European Consortium and dictated a letter containing three questions – a letter which was to be sent back to him at the ministry of defence. When 'Horne's' letter arrived, Heseltine sent his carefully prepared answer. The first of the three questions was whether the ministry of defence would buy Black Hawk. Heseltine's reply said that 'the government has no intention of procuring Black Hawk'. The second question was whether Westland had ever exported a helicopter that had not first been purchased by the British military. Heseltine replied, 'I am advised there has been no such export.' Finally the letter asked what projects in Europe 'further to the Prime Minister's letter' might be lost to Westland if it undertook the Sikorsky deal. Heseltine said:

There are three further helicopters intended to form the core of the fleet of the British armed forces in the longer term, all of which are planned to be produced collaboratively. . . . [These were the battlefield helicopter, the transport helicopter (the NH90), and the big naval EH101 with Agusta.] There are indications available to HMG both from the other governments and the companies concerned that a Westland link with Sikorsky/Fiat would be incompatible with participation by that company on behalf of the UK in the collaborative battlefield helicopter and NH90 projects. There have been separate indications from Agusta that if the Westland deal with Sikorsky went through, Agusta would have to seek other partners.

This second letter was a piece of gamesmanship. Heseltine was probably on firm ground in asserting the demise of the battlefield project and the NH90; the EH101 was likely to survive a Sikorsky deal. It was sharp practice. Heseltine's justification for his riposte was that Cuckney had ignored in his public statements all the qualifications which Heseltine had inserted in the Prime Minister's letter.

Thirty, fifteen.

The third letter is, of course, the one for which the whole Westland Affair will long be remembered. Mrs Thatcher was angry. On the Friday evening there was a meeting at Number 10 at which Mrs Thatcher and her aides, having gone through the second letter line by line, determined on yet another counterattack. It was Mrs Thatcher's turn to speak of 'material inaccuracies'. The scheme was to persuade the solicitor general to write a letter pointing out that there had been such inaccuracies.

Mrs Thatcher instructed Sir Patrick Mayhew, Downing Street having discussed the matter with the DTI, to prepare such a letter. Having received his instructions late on the Saturday night, Mayhew rang Heseltine to tell him that the second letter 'went too far'. 'It doesn't go far enough,' was Heseltine's answer. There was to be an exchange of letters on the Monday.

Over the weekend of 4 and 5 January the Prime Minister discussed tactics with Lord Whitelaw and John Wakeham at Chequers. The Prime Minister is believed to have told her colleagues of Mayhew's intention to write a letter pointing out that there had been 'material inaccuracies'. It was finally decided that an ultimatum was to be given to Heseltine on the following Thursday morning at the regular meeting of the cabinet. He was forbidden to make any more public statements whatever about Westland unless he submitted them for approval in advance by the cabinet office. George Younger, the secretary of state for Scotland, was designated as Heseltine's replacement at defence (although he was not sounded out in advance).

The events that followed have been well documented. Mayhew wrote his letter:

> . . . on the basis of the information contained in the documents to which I have referred, which I emphasise are all that I have seen, the sentence in your letter to Mr Horne does in my opinion contain material inaccuracies in the respect I have mentioned and I therefore must advise you that you should write again to Mr Horne correcting the inaccuracies.

Had the matter stopped there, with no selective leak of the contents of a confidential letter from a law officer, Heseltine would have been obliged to respond publicly in one way or another. But the passions which had been raised by the affair were running too strongly; the rules were bent, with consequences for Mrs Thatcher and her government that are still incalculable.

The letter was leaked on the Monday. Mrs Thatcher was later to say that there had been a 'misunderstanding' between officials at Downing Street and officials at the department of trade and industry. There was to be a clash of views over how the leak had happened. The versions given by Number 10 to Sir Robert Armstrong during his inquiry did not tally with what Colette Bowe had testified. Armstrong interviewed Bowe on two occasions. Mrs Thatcher eventually reported to the House that there had been a misunderstanding between them over the authorisation of the leak. Ingham maintained that when he talked to Bowe he was 'reluctantly' accepting a leak which had already been proposed by the department of trade and industry. Colette Bowe, a DTI official, maintained that it was Ingham who insisted that the leak must come from the DTI and not from Number 10, and had proposed the method by which it should be done. Bowe also believed that her permanent secretary, Sir John Mogg, had already cleared it with Number 10. In short, a bugger's muddle.

Mayhew's anger when he discovered that he had been 'used' in this way, was great. He threatened resignation. He wrote immediately to Heseltine: 'I want to express my dismay that a letter containing confidential legal advice from a law officer to one of his colleagues should have been leaked, and leaked, moreover in a highly selective way. . .this important rule was immediately and flagrantly violated.' Mayhew went on to add a passage which was helpful to Heseltine's position:

> The additional evidential material on which you rely, and in particular the conversations with your European colleagues to which you referred, is identified to me in your letter in terms too general for me to be able personally to assess whether the accuracy test is fulfilled. I quite understand why this may be unavoidable, particularly in the case of the conversations with your European colleagues, but it means that the judgement as to whether the test is satisfied must remain your own responsibility.

Heseltine, far from retracting, issued a public repeat of his original statement to the European Consortium and stood by his words.

Thus the exchange of the three letters constituted an 'escalation' of the affair, with each of the contestants in turn being prepared to go to greater lengths to disconcert the other. In the end, it was either Downing Street or the DTI (or both) that was responsible for an unscrupulous and clumsy manoeuvre which laid a charge beneath Heseltine which blew up in the Prime Minister's face. The leak to the Press Association was an obvious plant. It was also clear that the full text of the letter was less than sensational, or it would have been leaked verbatim.

On Friday 3 January 1986, six days before his resignation, I went to see Michael at the ministry of defence. As one of the three vice-chairmen of the party's Defence Committee, I had access to him. We talked for fifteen minutes or so, and I told him that the 'defence interest' among Tory backbenchers was on his side. But few Tory MPs nowadays take an interest in defence; politics is about economics. I warned him against resignation, using the argument that he could oppose Margaret more effectively from within the cabinet. At the mention of the Prime Minister, he said wryly that I didn't know the half of it. I found him tense, and clearly under great strain. When I left him I passed Jim Prior in the corridor wearing his General Electric Company hat, and Sir Raymond Lygo in his British Aerospace blazer. The ministry of defence was on a war footing. I felt, having seen Michael, that his resignation was inevitable. No one, however, could have foretold the extraordinary circumstances that surrounded the event.

In retrospect, Heseltine's resignation could only have been a matter of time. After the episode of the three letters, and Leon Brittan's public dispute with Sir Raymond Lygo over the rival interpretations given to the meeting between them, the state of undeclared war which existed between Heseltine on the one side, and Mrs Thatcher and Leon Brittan on the other, could lead only to Armageddon. Nevertheless, we were all taken by surprise.

Heseltine thought the cabinet on Thursday 9 January would be unremarkable. He told his wife that there was no question of his resignation. He told a Tory backbencher who had worked closely with him throughout the affair, in a conversation that took place the night before, that Westland 'was not on the agenda'. If the topic were to be raised, Heseltine would fall back to his previous position, namely, that he would be obliged to answer questions on the affair, if asked. 'There won't be a row.' The same ally rang him next morning at the ministry of defence and said to him, 'We are quite clear that, whatever happens, you are not going to resign today?' Heseltine replied, 'We are quite clear.'

As everyone knows, Mrs Thatcher, by taking out of her

bag the letter which she and her intimates had concocted over the weekend at Chequers, and demanding that all future comment should be cleared by her office in advance, precipitated Heseltine's resignation. Norman Tebbit, the chairman of the party, tried to buy time; he was clearly concerned to limit the political damage. Heseltine did not have time to consider what response he should make, or what action he should take; the discussion was brief and summed up by the Prime Minister. It was then that Heseltine gathered his papers together, stood up, said, 'I cannot accept that decision', and walked out. No one tried to stop him. Whitelaw might have tried, but he did nothing. For a moment at least, Mrs Thatcher was rendered speechless. The meeting adjourned for coffee and chocolate biscuits.

For Heseltine, the Celt had taken over from the calculator. Samson-like, he kicked out at the columns of the temple, bringing the roof down on the head of the Prime Minister, and burying them both in the rubble. Prime ministers have had to put up with ministerial resignations in the past, but none has been so publicly humiliated. The clip of film, taken outside Downing Street that morning, in which Heseltine says to camera, 'I've resigned from the cabinet and shall be making a full statement later on', and then strides out of the picture, lies easily at hand in the television archives. The Westland Affair, which had not lacked drama, had been given a high note which was not to be obscured even by the sight and sound of a Prime Minister at bay.

The next twenty-four hours saw Heseltine rarely off the screen. The story spread that he had appeared six times on television that day, wearing six different ties. Like many good stories, this was untrue; throughout January Heseltine wore his favourite, the blue and red stripes of the Brigade of Guards.

The Times leader described the resignation as 'stylish', which was as good a word as any. Geoffrey Smith, who writes a low-key but sensible column in that newspaper, wrote on 9 January:

. . . many of those who agree with him on the substance, including a number of his ministerial colleagues, believe that he is overplaying his hand. They are not suggesting that he is bidding for the leadership. . .all the signs are that throughout this dispute, Mr Heseltine has been acting as an angry man rather than as a personally calculating man. There have been three distinct phases in the political reactions to his campaign. First, there was a sense of astonishment, mingled with awe, at the risk he was running. Then mounting admiration for his nerve and accomplishment in securing a hearing for the European option – to the point where it seems that his stature would be enhanced whatever the outcome. Now there is quite a widespread feeling that he has been throwing more punches than have been necessary for his cause. But it is not only Mr Heseltine who has ignored the cabinet's ruling on restraint. Leon Brittan has also been battling away with much vigour, even if his tactics have less the flavour of a cavalry charge.

Times columnists are free to mix their metaphors, but I do like Smith's last sentence. Brittan has never seen a horse; he was a sapper and miner.

We Tories held our breath. Heseltine's friends were alarmed at what we saw as his recklessness. His enemies exulted. Heseltine, they claimed, 'had burnt his boats'. Those who were uncommitted saw that Heseltine's challenge to the Prime Minister, motivated as it was, in part, by personal animus, could not be permitted to succeed. Like it or not, Mrs Thatcher was Prime Minister. Her government, and the party, could only be in danger. The area whips, at the prompting of their chief, telephoned their flock with the intention of steadying the sheep. With our ear to the telephone, we followed the exploits of Heseltine upon the box. Having spent the afternoon of the 9th at the ministry writing a resignation statement of two and a half thousand words, Heseltine justified his action on two grounds: Mrs Thatcher's disregard for cabinet government, and the wisdom of a European alternative to Sikorsky. The nation watched as he even took to the skies in a French helicopter for the benefit of Channel 4.

Politicians spoke of nothing else but Heseltine's resignation. Heseltine himself seemed to have recognised the extent of his gamble, admitting, somewhat wryly, that 'he who wields the dagger never wears the crown' – and most of his party colleagues would still agree with him. Some thought the issue on which he had fought to have been of little importance ('Who cares about helicopters anyway?'); others felt his tactics to have been outrageous, and that faced with so obvious a challenge, Mrs Thatcher had to react strongly or face charges of pusillanimity. His friends felt he had 'gone over the top'. All in politics, of whatever party, backbencher and commentator, relished the excitement.

The public, on the other hand, warmed to him. The affair was seen to have been the making of Heseltine. Until then only the intelligentsia and the Conservative Party political activists had any clear image of him. For the rest he was just a better-looking politician than the others. The man on the Bradford omnibus had a clear picture of Mrs Thatcher; as for her cabinet colleagues, they seemed, in the main, to consist of faceless people called Norman and Kenneth. Politicians are inclined to assume that the occasional appearance on 'Newsnight' guarantees fame, but the opinion polls suggest otherwise. The really famous are the television and showbusiness celebrities: even Cecil Parkinson is less well known than Michael. By his resignation, Heseltine achieved fame, something which he had long and assiduously sought. He had the additional satisfaction to be derived from the public's opinion. Only 17% believed the government's version of events to have been truthful: 72% did not. A majority thought Heseltine had been right to resign.

As a Tory backbencher and an officer of the party's Defence Committee I was a privileged spectator of the Westland Affair. Hindsight encourages compression; events, as they unfolded during December and January, did not always fit neatly into a pattern. We followed the tortuous course of the affair with the help of the newspapers, the encouragement of gossip, which was to be derived from MPs closer to either Heseltine or Brittan than I was, and from the occasional parliamentary appearance of the principals. As the affair progressed so the drama moved from behind the closed doors of Whitehall to Westminster. In a sense it was a battle of the parliamentary private secretaries, MPs with their foot on the lowest rung of the ladder, who were busily at work pedalling their masters' lines. Gerry Malone, a clever and engaging Scot, spoke up for Leon Brittan; Keith Hampson and Nicholas Baker for Michael Heseltine. All three could be seen frequently holding court in the members' lobby, whispering intently to politician and correspondent alike.

In fact, most of us were partly privileged spectators. The cabinet tries to control the information it releases through the 'unattributable' daily lobby briefing of correspondents, presided over by Bernard Ingham. The party whips, many of whom seemed to age during the affair, are seekers after the opinions of their flock; only when the government has a case to defend or a point of view to advance, do the whips proselytise on its behalf. In the early stages the whips were as bewildered as everyone else. The members' lobby became a market for information, where the seekers after truth bargained the one with the other in search of that most precious of commodities, news. We were never briefed; but we were capable of taking sides.

We could take little that was fresh back to our constituents, save partisanship. Heseltine called upon the support of his friends only to find them disappointingly few in number. Brittan's were an even more select band. Among Tories, Colonel Mates, the Member for East Hampshire, was perhaps Heseltine's stoutest supporter. He was then a member of the Commons Select Committee on Defence – he has since become its chairman. But it was curious, given the public prominence of the two rival cabinet ministers, that Tory MPs were slow to join the colours.

Heseltine had never been closely identified with Mrs Thatcher's opponents – the 'wets' adopted an attitude of benevolent neutrality towards him, while relishing the evident discomfiture of the Prime Minister. Leon Brittan had to make do with those who would automatically rally to Mrs Thatcher's banner, however tattered, a band of the brave which had shrunk in size, having suffered from disaffection and desertion. As the glass dropped fast, the majority of Conservative MPs opted to play the role for which nature has conceived them, that of the party's ballast.

The 1922 Committee, which ministers can attend though they must keep silent, came into its own at the end of the Westland Affair. Its chairman is Cranley Onslow, the MP for Woking, a Tory with a sense of humour. I usually avoid the Thursday evening meeting. Too frequent an attendance can result in what religious people call 'doubts'. Mostly it consists of the desultory reading by one of the party whips of the next week's business, followed by a question or two; very occasionally it becomes a theatre, either of cruelty or of the absurd.

The meeting of the '22' on the evening of 23 January 1986 followed on the heels of Mrs Thatcher's very unsatisfactory statement made earlier that afternoon. At 3.30 p.m. she had announced that the department of trade and industry had authorised the leak from the Mayhew letter with the knowledge of Number 10. She claimed she had been unaware of the decision to leak but approved of it in retrospect. She said she had been given the full facts only the day before, sixteen days after the leak occurred. Neil Kinnock called for an emergency debate which was later scheduled for the next Monday. It was on the 23rd he coined his most memorable phrase of the affair: 'government not only rotten to the core, but rotten from the core'. More effective, if less grandiloquent, was Tory ex-Minister Alex Fletcher's question to the Prime Minister, 'Are you satisfied the statement you made this afternoon has enhanced the integrity of the government?' For a second time that month, Mrs Thatcher was reduced to silence.

At six that evening two hundred backbenchers made for committee-room 14. It was going to be too good to miss. A full hall, an issue of much moment, events of high drama and a ready-made victim; even the smoking-room was deserted. I broke the rule of a lifetime and turned up.

The '22' that evening brought back memories of the Profumo Affair twenty years earlier, when, faced with a crisis of the same magnitude (and historical unimportance), the Tory Party ran screaming from side to side of the sinking ship before tossing Harold Macmillan over the side in an act of propitiation.

It is, of course, in times of crisis such as Profumo, the Falklands War and the Westland Leak that the Conservative backbencher, generally regarded as the lowest form of political life, comes into his own. A routine meeting, frowsy and somnolent, turns, as if by magic, into a kangaroo court where the accused is tried without benefit of counsel, condemned by the voices of the unregarded and sentenced to political oblivion. The sight and sound of the '22' with its blood up is not one for the squeamish.

Twenty years or more ago, Harold Macmillan would occasionally be invited to address the committee. He would stand before it nervously fingering his Brigade tie, certain in the knowledge that he was among friends. Lord Carrington's career was destroyed by the pack in full cry. After the extraordinary Saturday morning debate in April 1982, which took place immediately after the capture of the Falklands, the foreign secretary climbed the stairs to the committee corridor summoned not by bells but by the officers of the party's Defence and Foreign Affairs Committees. The bulk of the party turned up to see the fun, some rendered hysterical through humiliation. It was rather like the nastier bits in *Tom Brown's Schooldays*.

Carrington was betrayed in part by his arrogance, in part

162

by his unfamiliarity, as a peer, with our little ways. He should have spoken at length, taking some of the blame for which he was later exonerated, and threatening retribution on General Galtieri. Five minutes might have been left for questions. Instead he said to the officers as he climbed the rostrum, 'If the buggers want my resignation, they can have it', and tossed down the gauntlet by speaking briefly, thus allowing the floor thirty minutes for questions. Leon Brittan's trial *in absentia* was in the great tradition.

Brittan was to be the necessary sacrifice. Mrs Thatcher's statement that afternoon had, for all its equivocation, fingered her secretary of state. She may have tried to protect him but the result was to leave him naked to his enemies. The atmosphere in the committee room was highly charged. Usually the colleagues sit quietly, nice old things in old-fashioned suits, men who correspond monthly with aged kinsmen, appear on breakfast television, and never cheat. The meetings are good natured and the humour largely unconscious. Instructions to remain in to the small hours at the beck and call of some junior ministerial colleagues are accepted with a good grace, while the 'whip on duty' is made welcome. A member might raise the matter of pigs or the need for a bypass. By ten past six we are back in the smoking-room.

But it was not to be on that evening. Poor Leon had no credit in the bank. He had fought his mistress's corner but to no avail. Over the matter of the receipt of the letter from Sir Austin Pearce, chairman of British Aerospace, marked 'private and confidential', Mrs Thatcher who had been sitting next to him on the treasury bench, might have saved him with a word. His intelligence, the swiftness of his promotion, his dogged loyalty, his benefit of patronage, and his religion (one rumbustious Tory backbencher had already called on television for his successor to be 'a red-faced Englishman') stood him in no stead. He was at the mercy of the tongues of five or six of his colleagues and condemned by the silence of many others. When the hanging was over, Cranley

Onslow, who had done nothing to encourage the mob, left to find the chief whip with the opinion that Brittan Must Go.

Later that evening there were rumours to the effect that 'Leon will spill the beans'. But he did not. Instead he resigned on the following day, disregarding Mrs Thatcher's efforts to persuade him to stay put. His speeches since on Westland have been devoted to attacking Heseltine's part in the affair. He has said nothing about Mrs Thatcher's part in the leaking of the Mayhew letter. She has promised that he will, one day, return to office, an undertaking already given to Cecil Parkinson. Brittan has not returned to the Bar, but has joined a small merchant bank. While Heseltine has been busily engaged in mending his fences, Brittan has, save for a speech on the Peacock Committee on broadcasting, which he set up when home secretary, been treading water. Unlike Cecil and the disgraced Jeffrey Archer, he was not invited to Christmas lunch at Chequers in 1986 by Mrs Thatcher.

Not unsurprisingly, Michael wasn't asked for turkey and pud. either. Did he completely mishandle the Westland business? How skilful or otherwise a political operator did the affair reveal him to be?

Sir Frank Cooper, one of the best-informed of the Westland watchers, claims that Heseltine lacks subtlety. When he did finally 'pick up the ball and start running with it', it was too late and his 'handling of it, too blatant'. A more skilful politician would have resorted, according to Cooper, to 'wheeler-dealing'; that is, he would have worked more assiduously upon the views of his cabinet colleagues, and even upon Mrs Thatcher. This would have involved attempts to persuade his colleagues to his viewpoint (on the other hand, Norman Lamont, minister of state at defence, says Heseltine was never off the telephone), while at the same time instructing his civil servants to persuade their opposite numbers in other Whitehall departments. Sir Frank does not think that Heseltine ever throve on 'cut and thrust' arguments across the cabinet table. As one might expect, given Heseltine's well-known aversion to detail, he found such wrangling tedious and distasteful.

As we have seen, Heseltine was a great cinemagoer in his youth, with a taste for Westerns and for political dramas of the American kind. I think *All the King's Men*, the story of the rise and fall of the 'Kingfish', Huey Long, the governor of Louisiana, was a particular favourite. Long, incidentally, is remembered for this dictum: 'Always be sincere; even when you don't mean it.' However, there is nothing insincere about Michael. Heseltine must have gone into the cabinet room on Thursday 9 January taking with him something of Gary Cooper's integrity, although he resigned well before noon. His abortive attempt in the days before Christmas to do a deal with Cuckney owed more to Broderick Crawford's tycoon in *Born Yesterday*. It was a significant misjudgement of the man and the moment.

What are the qualities I admire in Michael Heseltine? As a manager, he seems to me to be superb; as a 'getter-up and doer', he has no equal in the Conservative Party. He works hard; he is dedicated; he is as straight as a die. When he wants something, he will work all hours to get it. There is nothing mean about the man or his politics. But he has his weaknesses.

Many will say that as secretary of state for defence, Heseltine was reluctant to take decisions, a wariness which might be put down to a lack of self-confidence, coming to defence as he did with no prior expertise. Or it could be attributed to a native caution that warned him of the political longevity of error. There is no doubt that his procrastination at the ministry of defence in '83 and '84 earned him the poor opinion of servicemen and civil servants alike.

Everyone who has had any dealing with him recognises the complexity of his character. He is an extremely private man. The recently elected among his colleagues complain that they do not know him. Which cannot be good politics on Michael's part. Michael Mates told me that on one occasion he gave Heseltine advice as to his prospects. The first thing, said Mates, 'is that nobody knows you. The second thing is some people don't trust you, and the third is you aren't around the place so people can't get to know you.' Heseltine's response was to the effect that he was not prepared to compromise his principles, which seems somehow to have missed the point.

It is significant that when Heseltine resigned, none of his ministerial team followed suit. John Lee was too junior; Norman Lamont, who had come to defence from trade and industry, was in sympathy with Leon Brittan's view, and, most surprising of all, John Stanley stayed put. Stanley is not a popular man either with his colleagues or his civil servants, and from time to time the press has carried unkind comment about him. He is humourless, but an immensely hard worker. 'He works all the hours God gave to do his Master's bidding.' Yet Stanley did not budge.

It was precisely Heseltine's lack of a personal following in the parliamentary party which allowed the Prime Minister to ride the storm caused by her prevarication and equivocation over the Westland Affair. As to the leaking of the Mayhew letter, whatever the truth behind it, she was inevitably criticised for the means employed. But had Heseltine been a popular figure within the Conservative Party, she and her government could not have survived his resignation and the circumstances surrounding it. The party cast itself in the role of a fascinated spectator of events as they unrolled; partisans were relatively few in number. Mrs Thatcher's enemies, and she has not a few among Tory MPs, warmed their hands at her discomfiture; Heseltine's friends, a smaller number than those who would consider themselves to be Margaret's enemies, did what they could for him, and his cause, before his resignation, but once it had happened, sat on their hands.

Tory MPs were not only stunned by Michael's announcement of resignation – never before has a cabinet minister flounced out of a meeting of the cabinet – they were taken by surprise. Although Heseltine's resignation had been discussed in the press, it had been discounted by every political

correspondent. His friends had warned him against so precipitate an action. In truth, Heseltine surprised himself.

The threat to the Conservative government, following
Heseltine's resignation, was not from Heseltine's supporters;
it was to Mrs Thatcher's reputation for integrity. Heseltine's
impotency was in part due to the Prime Minister's dominance
over her cabinet, most of her more obvious opponents having
been sacked from it, and in part to the suspicion with which
he (Heseltine) was regarded by many of his colleagues. A
glamorous 'loner' with a disconcertingly effective appeal to
the party activists at conferences, who appeared to some to
be rooted in no recognisably Tory tradition and to be
overweeningly ambitious, was not the kind of man to summon the Knights of Shire and Suburb to the barricade.
'Michael' said many of the stuffier party shirts at the time,
'has gone round the bend.'

I have no doubt that Michael, upon reflection, regretted his
resignation. He had stolen every headline, and, by his direct
attack upon the Prime Minister's style of leadership, done
much damage to Mrs Thatcher's already tarnished reputation. But she survived Westland because the bulk of the Tory
Party wanted her to do so. Loved by some and hated by
others, she enjoyed one overwhelming advantage; there was
no obvious successor to her.

In politics, does fortune favour the brave? 'Never resign' is
advice on a par with 'Never apologise, never explain.' Yet a
case can be made to the effect that those who are not
prepared to sink without trace do get to the top. I have called
it 'Rab's Law', after R.A. Butler's dictum. When asked why
he had never become prime minister, he replied that he had
never resigned. In order to climb the pole, or so it seems,
resignation is de rigueur.

Supporters of Rab's Law can point to Churchill, who was,
besides, forever changing parties. Anthony Eden resigned
over Munich. Harold Macmillan never resigned office, but he
did the next best thing, he resigned the party whip. In the
'thirties Macmillan was at one time considered by Attlee to

be the man most likely to lead the Labour Party. Heseltine's name has never been linked with membership of any other party.

After his resignation Heseltine was a spectator at events in which he had a bigger hand than most. While, in the wake of Westland, the government suffered from a failure of nerve over the future of the British motor industry, was defeated over Sunday trading and ran into rough water over the American attack on Libya, Heseltine took to the road to talk at meetings high and low about the things that interested him. At defence, George Younger was left to hold the fort by postponing all the more difficult decisions, save for the future of Britain's airborne early warning system, until the election. John Biffen went on television to call for a 'balanced ticket', and the government became embroiled in a court case in Australia over spies. At the end of the year the tide seemed to have turned in favour of the government. This was not caused by anything Mrs Thatcher and her ministers had done; Labour's defence policy and Alliance disagreements over defence had cut the support for both the opposition parties. Despite everything, the Conservative Party retains one immense advantage; the anti-Tory vote is split in two.

In December 1986 Norman Tebbit said on 'The David Frost Programme' that, 'Michael will have a major part to play at the election, particularly over defence.' Does rehabilitation lie this way?

Epilogue

What are the chances of Michael Heseltine achieving his life-long ambition of becoming Prime Minister? The odds must be against it. But the charm of politics lies in its unpredictability. Since Westland Heseltine has been assiduously mending fences. In January 1986 he opened the cocks of the Tory 'boat'; since then he has taken care not to rock it.

Even the party whips have said that Heseltine has, since Westland, 'behaved impeccably'. His speeches in the House have been 'helpful'. He may have savaged the poll tax in the debate on Second Reading of the Local Government Finance Bill in December 1987, but he finished his speech by attacking the Opposition, and took care not to vote against the Bill (as several of his colleagues did). He abstained.

Heseltine has gone into orbit. He travels the country ceaselessly on behalf of his friends and enemies, speaking for them tirelessly at annual dinners, taking as his text relatively uncontroversial but important topics such as inner-city regeneration and the future of the City of London. Those who would buy a copy of his credo *Where there is a Will* published in the spring of 1987 will catch the flavour of a hundred Tory dinners. All that is lacking is the taste of self-congratulation, overdone beef and tinned claret without which the party faithful are never at their best.

Having leapt so dramatically upon the Westland parapet, Heseltine is taking care to dig in. Just as a shovel is a vital part of an infantryman's equipment, so 'party loyalty' is to

Conservatives who would make good. At the election in the summer of 1987, Heseltine waged his own speaking campaign without the blessing of the party's Central Office. Any Tory who would aspire to become leader of his party has to walk the fine line between independence and disloyalty. Heseltine has demonstrated vividly his independence; since his resignation he has taken care not to give offence. His loyalty is not so much to Margaret, more to the party.

Tory prime ministers have first to be elected leader of the party, and the electorate consists of Tory MPs. In the past Heseltine, whose conference oratory has won him much support in the party beyond Westminster, has suggested that the franchise be widened to include the National Union, an unspecified number of the more prominent among the ranks of the party activists; but no voices were raised in his support. He has yet to return to this theme. It could be that Norman Tebbit, who has a prejudice to suit every member of the Conservative party, would poll more heavily than Heseltine in any such beauty contest. We Tories are unlikely to follow Labour down the road to party democracy.

The successor to Mrs Thatcher will be chosen by Tory MPs meeting in committee-room 14. Her hat trick of victories has confirmed the position of the Prime Minister and there is talk among her acolytes of 'a fourth term'. Those who are daunted by the prospect keep their counsel. Were she to retire, and it is believed that her husband, Denis, would like her to do so, or were she to die in harness, Heseltine, the backbencher, would find himself at a grave disadvantage. For as long as 'Maggie rules', Heseltine will languish on the front seat below the gangway. And the Prime Minister is an unforgiving woman. She is on record as having said 'I make up my mind about a person in ten seconds: rarely, if ever, do I change my mind.' Heseltine's chances of succeeding her would be greatly enhanced were the Conservatives to lose the next election.

It is easy enough to list Heseltine's rivals, but who are his friends? Heseltine has not spoken at the last two Tory party conferences. He might not have been called; and even had he been, ten minutes on the rostrum would not be long enough. He has, however, at Bournemouth in '86 and Blackpool in '87, spoken at fringe meetings organised by Tories who are sympathetic to him. At Bournemouth he spoke to a meeting sponsored by the leftish Tory Reform Group of which he is a patron. Heseltine had to make do with an audience of a thousand, one in four of the representatives at the conference. I sat in the hall wearing my journalist's hat.

Heseltine entered the hall surrounded by a posse of his friends. Tim Sainsbury, who before becoming first a whip and then a junior defence minister, was Michael's PPS – an appointment that gave rise to the comment that Michael, with the party to choose from, had picked the only one of his colleagues richer than himself; Keith Hampson, who had also been one of Michael's PPSs when Heseltine was at the ministry of defence, and Colonel Mates who has since become the chairman of the Defence Select Committee. Are three minders enough? At Blackpool, a year later, Heseltine spoke at a Tory Reform Group dinner. On both occasions he scooped the pool of publicity, thus upstaging the Conference proper.

Scratch a common or garden Tory MP and he bleeds loyalty. A hundred dinner table conversations chez Irving, the name which the irreverent have given the members' dining room as a tribute to Charles Irving, MP for Cheltenham Spa, and chairman of the Kitchen Committee, have given Heseltine some comfort. The predictable shake their grey heads and talk of boats. Many Tory MPs simply did not understand what Westland was about. What Heseltine saw as a point of principle, the party's footsoldiers saw as mutiny, an unparalleled act of self-indulgence carried out in the full view of the public. Thatcher loyalists will still not give him the time of day. When prompted, however, many Tories will pay tribute to Heseltine's political equipment, to the care with which he is mending fences, while the more far-sighted can see the vital part he might play in any Tory revival were they to be defeated at an election in 1991. Even so, many of the older Tories are worried as to his judgement.

The succession is a topic of great interest to Tories. It is thought to be faintly in bad taste, but such scruples are soluble in the house claret. Mrs Thatcher's eventual departure is an event about which some have allowed themselves to fantasise. A bright spring morning at Victoria Station where the Tory Party, drunk and sober, line platform 16 (the Dulwich line) in order to bid her farewell. Lord Whitelaw will say a few words. Ian Gow will be prevented from throwing himself beneath the wheels of the train, the driver of which will bear a resemblance to Sir Ian Gilmour. Lord Pym will have to be helped into the nearest waiting room. Prominent among the mourners will be the contenders for the Peacock Throne: Kenneth Baker, glossy and expectant; Peter Walker, fighting back a manly tear; Sir Geoffrey Howe, wearing shiny shoes; Norman Tebbit on his best behaviour, and Heseltine, wearing a black tie. Lord Young will carry her bags. As the train draws out of the station, Bernard Ingham will set fire to his uniform. The party will then disperse to the clubs of London where, over vintage champagne, the succession will be the topic on everyone's lips.

It may be fun to run through the qualities of the contenders. It must be borne in mind, however, that it will be hard for Heseltine to win the leadership from the back benches. His rivals are presently enjoying the advantages of stewardship. Some will no doubt stumble; most will derive benefit from their office. Electoral defeat would swiftly render the contenders equal for Mrs Thatcher would swiftly depart, and Heseltine would be unlikely to be excluded from any front bench role in opposition even with Mrs Thatcher still, nominally, in the saddle. Would defeat in 1991 mean a clean break with the past? Not if Norman Tebbit has anything to do with it.

As a Tory Democrat, Heseltine could be described as 'wet' at home and 'dry' abroad, a position which would not have been foreign to Churchill or Macmillan. Heseltine is pro-

Europe. He takes a robustly pro-Nato, and therefore pro-nuclear line. Whatever the merit of the arguments, no contender for the Tory leadership could fail to take a hard line on defence. His rivals can claim to hold similar views, but Heseltine has the advantage of the reputation and expertise he acquired in his three years as secretary of state for defence.

Although none of his eight predecessors at defence became prime minister (one has to go as far back as Harold Macmillan's brief tenure in the 'fifties), the office is a card which none of his rivals can play. Tebbit knows more about attack than defence. Kenneth Baker knows nothing about the subject. Peter Walker was for a few months under Ted Heath the shadow defence spokesman, but he cannot speak any longer with authority on defence matters. Biffen has had nothing to do with the subject (what is more he is believed to be agnostic about Trident), and neither has Lawson or Douglas Hurd. Heseltine can play the patriot with more vigour than his rivals.

Since my election to Parliament as Member for Rochester and Chatham in 1959, I have sat at the feet of four Tory leaders. I was, of course, a spectator at the elevation of Harold Macmillan in 1957. In 1963, when the election of the leader was still the function of the 'magic circle', I nervously wrote a letter to the then chief whip, Martin Redmayne (he ended his days working at Harrods), tentatively suggesting that Rab Butler was best equipped to succeed Harold Macmillan. I received an acknowledgment in due course. Sadly, I was not in the House for the leadership contest of 1965 after Sir Alec, by removing his hat, did the decent thing. I had lost my seat.

Heath was preferred to Reggie Maudling not because of policy difference between the two men, but on grounds of prowess and personality. Maudling was judged by some to be too idle; Heath appeared to many to be more in tune with the times, the man to take on Harold Wilson. Edward Boyle told me that on the day after the election, he had gone into the smoking-room before lunch to find Reggie Maudling seated before a gin and tonic. 'What have I to look forward to but to sit here and get pissed?' said Reggie. Which was precisely what he did. How sad that so gifted a man, and so young – he was still in his forties – should have felt that way. But the point is not the bitterness of defeat, which is never absent, but the lack of ideological content. It was not until Margaret Thatcher defeated Ted Heath and went on to win the leadership of the party on the second ballot, that a policy dimension entered into the contest. In 1963 and in 1965 there was no 'right wing' candidate. In 1975 there was, and she won. The next contest will assuredly divide along ideological lines.

As a Tory Democrat, Heseltine would be but one of several candidates in the moderate interest. The right wing which dominated the Conservative Party under Neville Chamberlain, and does now under Mrs Thatcher, can look to three possible standard bearers. The moderates, those Tories who doubt if the free market contains within it a moral dimension, could field five players. A stand off between left and right might leave John Biffen, perhaps the most interesting and attractive Tory of them all, once a radical, then a 'consolidator', in a strong position. He has said that he will not go out of his way to make life easy for Mrs Thatcher, and there is no love lost between them. His chance could come were the rivals to cancel each other out. But there are those who wonder whether he would have the stomach for the fight.

Leon Brittan is one right-winger whose chances must be discounted. His hopes must lie in redemption; his return to the cabinet, the gift of a grateful Mrs Thatcher for whom he was prepared to lay down his life. Who was it who said that there is no gratitude in politics? Leon still languishes on the back benches. He has no power base: a clever man who was the victim of the party's need to find a scapegoat, he has paid a high price for his support of the Prime Minister.

We should not forget Cecil Parkinson. Raised from the dead by Mrs Thatcher, he is now the secretary of state for energy. He is an engaging man who has reason to claim, along with Marlon Brando in the film *On the Waterfront* that, he, too, 'could have been a contender'. Had Cecil been a minister of the Third Republic, the 'Parkinson Affair' could have made him the President of the Republic. In England, sadly, he has become a cautionary tale: the victim of love, indiscretion and the moral rectitude of Fleet Street. Yet Cecil could come again.

Who, then, will be the standard bearers of the Conservative right? They are Norman Tebbit, Nigel Lawson and Geoffrey Howe. The moderate contenders must include Kenneth Baker, Peter Walker, George Younger, Douglas Hurd and Michael Heseltine. Before returning to Heseltine I shall examine the credentials of the other seven. If we adopt the technique of the beauty competition and begin with the least attractive, one is obliged to start with Nigel Lawson.

Nigel Lawson's stock has been rising fast, although from what his Treasury advisors would call 'a low base'. He has been Chancellor for five years, and his 1988 budget earned him the gratitude of every Tory MP who paid tax at the top rate. He is blessed with a powerful intellect and a suitably bullying manner. He does have a talent to offend. No one has ever doubted his competence. His enemies are not silent. In the words of one of his cabinet colleagues (and a fellow contender) 'he fails the Enoch Powell tiger test', that is, he is not regarded as the sort of man with whom it would be sensible to go tiger hunting. 'It would not be the tiger's head that ended up fixed to the wall.' There is no friendship at the top. Charity is a quality we Tories leave to the Church of England, an organisation of which our leaders have come to disapprove.

Lawson is his own man. He is also the only cabinet minister ever to have told Mrs Thatcher to shut up. This act of lese-majesty happened in cabinet when the Prime Minister insisted upon continually interrupting the unfortunate Sir Keith Joseph, not permitting him to string together more than three words at a time. She coloured up, and for fifteen minutes kept silent. Fortune may favour the brave. I suppose were he to be offered the leadership, he would accept it, but it does seem more likely that he will quit politics for the City after the 1989 budget. He might, however, be the man for whom Norman Tebbit is looking.

We come, therefore, to Tebbit and Howe. Tebbit is the best body puncher in politics; like Lloyd George he has only to see a belt in order to hit below it. He does not always discriminate between his friends and his enemies. He is capable of describing the 127 Tories who did not support the restoration of capital punishment in the last Parliament as a mere 'handful', and of giving his endorsement to an organisation such as Recap, which is pledged to campaign against his colleagues in the party. He has strongly denied saying that 'no one with a conscience votes Tory', and I believe him. Like Mrs Thatcher herself, it is hard to be neutral about Tebbit.

As a Conservative, Tebbit is a fundamentalist with a wicked tongue. Cavernous in appearance, mordant of wit and divisive of opinion, he would appeal only to the right of the parliamentary party. A recently held poll had Tebbit the favourite among Tory party activists; Heseltine the favourite of the public at large. Nevertheless, he would be a high risk candidate; 'he would be worse than Margaret' is a view I have heard expressed. Sympathy for him following his injuries incurred in the Brighton bombing, and the sad condition of his wife, is widespread. He is a courageous man.

He, too, has fallen out with Margaret. Mrs Thatcher had a bad election but a good result. The story of 'wobbly Thursday', the day during the campaign when it looked for a moment as if Labour were about to recover, is well-known. Wracked by an abcess on her tooth and suffering from an attack of nerves, Mrs Thatcher blamed Central Office and the party chairman, Norman Tebbit. Voices were raised but best faces put forward. After the election, Tebbit surprised everyone by refusing high office and returning to the back benches.

Was this a case of *reculer pour mieux sauter*? In a newspaper interview published in the spring of 1988, Tebbit said that he was not a candidate for the leadership but that he might move were Mrs Thatcher's successor not to be to his liking. Who then does he consider to be worthy of bearing the sacred flame? Norman Tebbit is clearly leaving his choices open. We can be certain that Heseltine is not seen by Tebbit as a proper torch-bearer. His alliance with Heseltine in February 1988 when together they tabled a Commons Early Day Motion demanding the abolition of the Inner London Education Authority, which was gratefully accepted by Kenneth Baker and subsequently passed into law, was a marriage of convenience between beauty and the beast.

It could be that Tebbit has offended too many of his colleagues ever to win the leadership of the party. His popularity among constituency Conservatives, many of whom see him as the champion of the so-called 'moral majority', does not outweigh the apprehension of his Westminster colleagues. And it is we who vote. The party's right wing will look for a candidate whose appeal goes beyond the narrow confines of the right itself: that candidate can only be Sir Geoffrey Howe.

Geoffrey Howe is a lovely man. He has been described as the nicest, and as the most boring man in Europe. If he is dull it is only when he is on his feet. Had Mrs Thatcher retired hurt after Westland, Geoffrey would, in all probability, have inherited her mantle. Her retirement between now and 1991 would deny Howe so comfortable a transfer.

His strengths include his intelligence and his durability. Generously proportioned, rumpled and good-natured, Howe has been, on occasion, badly treated by the Prime Minister. He has had to suffer her rough tongue, but he has, over the years developed a technique which allows him to cope. He remains totally unruffled and returns doggedly to the point he is trying to make. He has had also to endure over the years the ridicule of Denis Healey. Howe has thus demonstrated an unrivalled ability to absorb punishment, to go the distance. He is not a fundamentalist, as is Tebbit. He is on the traditional right of the Conservative party where decency is placed above doctrine and sensitivity above resolution.

177

Howe was perhaps an undistinguished chancellor, who did his Mistress's bidding, allowing the pound to rise too high and thus deepening the recession. The 'wets' may hold that against him. But he has been a distinguished foreign secretary. His friends have suggested that Howe would be the ideal man for 'a doctor's mandate' (the country being safe in the hands of 'Dr' Howe): those who would look for a rougher ride remember Harold Macmillan's nickname of 'the anaesthetist'. Geoffrey is a man without enemies; whether he would have enough friends to win a leadership election may be doubted. For Howe an election cannot come quickly enough.

It is hard to remember all the names of those who have served in Mrs Thatcher's many cabinets but it is impossible to overlook John Biffen. He was once a nationalist, who, owing to his close friendship with Enoch Powell in the 'seventies, became known as 'John the Baptist'. As Powell faded into a passionate obscurity, Biffen transferred his affections to Mrs Thatcher, but his ardour was to cool. He took against her self-righteousness. After his call on 'Weekend World' in May 1986 for a balanced ticket, which was one way of saying let us have less of the Prime Minister and more of her ministers, Biffen was described by Charles Moore of the *Spectator* as 'Margaret's Judas'. John has now played two parts in the New Testament and is presently in the Wilderness.

His move away from the right towards the party's centre has been recognised by his colleagues. The fact that he is no longer 'one of us' could extend his appeal across the party. As Leader of the House his courtesy and wit made him the most popular boy in the school, winning the admiration of politician and journalist alike. There remains one question mark: his stamina. Could he stand the pace? Freneticism has become, for Prime Ministers at least, the order of the day. He is certainly no workaholic. Biffen may not actively seek the party leadership but he could find it nonetheless. Whosoever the next leader may turn out to be, Biffen will not stay unemployed.

Among the Tory moderates or 'consolidators' as John

Biffen has called them, Kenneth Baker and George Younger are Heseltine's most formidable rivals. Lord Whitelaw's retirement following his mild stroke has removed one, at least, of Heseltine's enemies. Perhaps it is the contempt of old money for new? There are those who claim that had he intervened at the moment of Heseltine's walk-out on 9 January 1986, he might have prevented his resignation. In the event, once the door had slammed behind the departing Heseltine, there was a stunned silence which lasted some minutes. Whitelaw was asked to find out what had happened. He left the room only to glimpse Heseltine standing in the street outside before a battery of cameras. Whitelaw could not abide Heseltine whom he has been heard to describe as 'the sort of man who combs his hair in public.' Today he seems to have changed his mind.

Baker and Younger, unlike Heseltine, lack enemies. This is not true of Peter Walker who has, over the years, acquired a good few. Walker and Heseltine have been friends for twenty years. They formed a political partnership of sorts in the late 'sixties, after Michael's election to the House for Tavistock. They are birds of a feather, although Walker is a working-class boy who rose through the chairmanship of the Young Conservative Movement to Westminster. En route, he, too, made money, in his case through insurance and property, although not quite as much as Heseltine. Walker abandoned Slater before the latter's downfall. A competent, although not a brilliant speaker, Walker has Heseltine's stamina and dedication to the minutiae of politics, for he, too, is a great traveller on behalf of his friends, and he can boast unbroken service in Mrs Thatcher's cabinets, despite a mutual antipathy.

When it comes to Peter, Mrs Thatcher has always been guided by her second thoughts. Although she would never put it this way, she has acted on Lyndon Johnson's dictum that it is better to have X inside the tent pissing out, than outside the tent pissing in. Peter Walker's running battle against 'Thatcherism' within the cabinet and his lightly coded critical speeches beyond it, have served to polarise the opinion of him held by Tory MPs. The right would die in the ditch to prevent him from taking the leadership; the left has a choice between champions.

Mrs Thatcher sent Walker into exile in Wales. Peter was right to have accepted her offer. Before the election when he was secretary of state for energy he was excluded from membership of the more important cabinet committees. As secretary of state for Wales he sits on them all. Walker's flair for public relations, and the fact that he has been given a free hand in his fiefdom, promises to make him an outstandingly successful Welsh secretary. He would have found the back benches full to overflowing with the dismissed.

George Younger has only recently achieved the status of a contender. The defeat of Teddy Taylor, the shadow Scottish secretary, on the streets of Cathcart in the 1979 election propelled George into the cabinet. Taylor fled south to Southend where he took refuge among the seaside widows and where he has lived quietly ever since. After Heseltine flounced out of the cabinet, Mrs Thatcher took advantage of a break for coffee and chocolate biscuits to ask Younger whether he would swop Scotland for defence. George, who is no stranger to good fortune, naturally accepted. He has proved to be a competent secretary of state who has given his ministry a welcome period of peace and quiet. He has also come to be recognised as a sound performer both in the House and on the platform. He is good on the telly. George is a Scotsman without enemies, and no extremist. 'No one has ever called me a "Thatcherite"' is his boast. He has good manners, occupies a marginal seat and has a father who sits in the Lords.

Douglas Hurd is a grey man of formidable ability. He sounds too clever for the Conservative party. There is something about him of the Head Prefect. For as long as he remains at the Home Office where his task is to thwart the atavistic tendencies of his colleagues on front and back bench, he is unlikely to become a serious challenger. Which is a pity.

EPILOGUE

Kenneth Baker is the man of whom Michael Heseltine should be most afraid. As secretary of state for education, responsible for the Great Education Reform Bill ('gerbil' to its friends), he is in the happy position of a left-wing Tory doing things of which the centre and right of the party most heartily approve. As secretary of state for the environment he shone in comparison with his predecessor, Patrick Jenkin. No lover of Mrs Thatcher (he tends to charm her in cabinet by giving way to her in an extravagant fashion), or of her attitudes, his opposition to the temper of our times has been less obvious than his rivals'. Glossy (as is Heseltine), self-assured (Michael is nothing if not self-confident), literate (which Michael is not), and witty (which Heseltine is rarely), Baker is a politician to his forefinger, with one further advantage that Heseltine does not enjoy: he has been able, from the despatch box, to put a benign face on the government's policies. His rise has been startlingly swift, which has not yet prevented him from making more friends than enemies. When the question 'anything known' is asked of him by the unreconstructed right, Baker's charge sheet has less written on it than either Walker's or Heseltine's. He is perhaps too smooth for some. Edward Pearce has said of him 'I have seen the future and it smirks.' Pitted against Howe, Baker would stand the best chance of a moderate succeeding Mrs Thatcher as the leader of our great party.

But timing is everything. Were Mrs Thatcher to drop dead, the succession would be fought out between Howe and Baker. Were she to retire after defeat at the general election, Heseltine would be a contender. Were she to win yet again, only to retire midway through the Fourth Term, then another generation of Tories might come into contention. John Major, the son of a trapeze artist, a numerate right-winger. John MacGregor, a clever Scot but without much magic. Chris Patten, the cleverest young man of them all, but suspected of having Jacobite sympathies. David Mellor, who has put the gunboat back into British diplomacy, having done for Israeli public opinion what Congressman Joe Kennedy managed to do for

181

ours during his fleeting visit to Northern Ireland. And we should not forget William Waldegrave.

Thus Michael Heseltine has an uphill task. What sort of party leader and prime minister would Heseltine make? As his unauthorised biographer I look for no reward, save the last governorship of the Falkland Islands. And that may already have been reserved for Leon Brittan. Mrs Thatcher who has never been satisfied with the last word, has set out to dominate her colleagues while keeping a high national 'profile'. Heseltine would attempt only the latter; his style has always been 'laid-back'; a Heseltine cabinet would not lack direction, but the term 'vegetable' would be unlikely ever to be applied to his colleagues. A post-Thatcher government and party might not pursue policies that were greatly different, but its tone of voice would have changed out of recognition. And all issues and events would have to be measured against Heseltine's known attitudes and prejudices.

He is a radical in the sense that he would reform by inter-vention and regulation what he sees as the unacceptable face of capitalism; he is a consolidator in the sense that he would pay heed to the needs of One Nation. As a Tory Democrat, he would give priority to the nation's security, and as a convinced European, he would place Britain's foreign policy in a European context. His social conscience, deriving as it does from his Welsh romanticism, makes him a cavalier; Mrs Thatcher born and bred in the eastern counties, is a roundhead.

The conventional wisdom has it that Heseltine cannot win from the back benches. Only Winston Churchill has leapt so far, but even he took two bounds, (he was made First Lord of the Admiralty, not Premier, on the outbreak of the Second World War), and he had the help of Adolf Hitler. Yet there is evidence to suggest that Heseltine might do it. A series of public opinion polls has suggested that the 1922 committee of Tory backbenchers rate him as 'the best backbencher', and make him the favourite to succeed. He is certainly setting the pace. At the time of the debate on the Mates Amendment on the Poll Tax in the spring of 1988, the newspapers carried the charge that the gallant Hampshire Colonel was no more than a stooge for Heseltine, a military monkey dancing to a Welsh organ-grinder's tune. This was nonsense. The suggestion could have come either from the press office of the Department of the Environment, a lobby briefing by the chief whip, David Waddington, or from a steer from the press office of No 10; a matter of Larry Ingham, Bernard Speaks. David Waddington is the most likely culprit.

It could well be that as the fortunes of Mrs Thatcher inexorably decline, so Heseltine's star will rise. He, at least, was not sacked by the Prime Minister; he walked out on her. Members of the cabinet asked him to speak at their annual constituency dinners, and he has been crossing and re-crossing the country speaking on behalf of less important Tories. His rivals in office do have the chance to make use of their position to attract attention. It could be that Heseltine's ceaseless activity will serve him just as well. He is not bound by convention and is free to pick, and discard, his themes, at will. He could take the two rival strands of modern Conservatism and weave from them a seamless robe, extending where we are into the future.

His particular task would be to attempt the regeneration of Britain's industrial and manufacturing base. To achieve this, he would dismantle what he calls 'the subsidies to the City of London' which are of the small, one-generation businesses at the hands of the Inland Revenue, the three billion pounds of mortgage relief which has underwritten the comparatively wealthy and, by the boom in insurance, made the institutional investor, with his short-term perspective, King of the City. England would become its own development area. An end would at last be brought to the forty-year old decline in British industry, a record which compares so poorly with our competitors. There is little doubt that such changes will be adopted by the post-Thatcher party, whether they are brought about by Heseltine or by a rival.

Heseltine is well qualified to lead. He could achieve his ambition and become Prime Minister. Much will depend upon the hour of Mrs Thatcher's departure. To reach No 10, Heseltine must get the better of The Dead Sheep, the Pole Cat and the Lounge Lizard. Whatever the result of the contest, I cannot wait to hear the sound of the bell for the first round.

Index

INDEX

ARMAND HAMMER
with Neil Lyndon

HAMMER: WITNESS TO HISTORY

'Readers will have to wait a long time for a busier life'
The Economist

An international legend in his own lifetime, Armand
Hammer is renowned as statesman, industrialist,
entrepreneur, philanthropist, collector – and much,
much more. Fom Lenin to Prince Charles, King Farouk
to Mrs Thatcher, Hammer has known and charmed
them all. But above all else, his is a story of Success.

'This exceptional book will arouse great interest all
over the world'

Menachem Begin

'an important perspective on many dramatic events'
Jimmy Carter

'This exercise in autobiography contains many a semi-
hidden jewel'

The Times Literary Supplement

A Royal Mail service in association with the Book Marketing Council & The Booksellers Association.
Post·A·Book is a Post Office trademark.

ANTHONY SUMMERS AND STEPHEN DORRIL

HONEYTRAP

A Conservative Minister for War and a Russian spy share the same mistress. There are daily revelations of bondage parties and of girls' cavorting at stately homes, of drugs and clubs, titled men and call girls. Some names are named. More are hinted at. Overnight, Christine Keeler and Mandy Rice-Davies are famous; the public fascinated.

The Minister, John Profumo, resigns. But the Establishment closes ranks and Dr Stephen Ward, the society doctor and artist who had made the introductions, is hounded to suicide.

Only a fraction of the truth was told at the time. Now *Honeytrap* reveals that the real story was even more sensational, that the British scandal even threatened to bring down President Kennedy in the United States.

'Bulging with new material . . . This is a book which our rulers must loathe'

Tribune

'Reopens the case and once again we are left suspecting that we do indeed live in a secret society'

Women's Journal

'Debauchery, class antagonism and espionage, a potent formula for a bestseller'

Irish Times

HODDER AND STOUGHTON PAPERBACKS

DICK WILSON

THE SUN AT NOON

Hard to understand and too important to ignore, Japan is a constant object of envy, irritation, puzzlement, admiration and curiosity.

Where are the Japanese heading? Are they moving closer to the West or are they turning in on themselves and rediscovering their own culture? What *is* the relationship between the traditional Japan, and the recent, seemingly Westernised Japan? How will it all affect us?

Award-winning journalist and author Dick Wilson has made forty visits to Japan since 1953. His understanding of the place and its people is unique. His enthusiasm is communicated straight to the reader in his lively and fascinating book, packed with facts, analysis and impressions.

'An essential read'

Accountancy

'A convincing account of modern Japan'
The Economist

'An admirably fair-minded objectivity in his judgements'

Hampstead & Highgate Express

HODDER AND STOUGHTON PAPERBACKS

BRIAN HARPUR

THE IMPOSSIBLE VICTORY

At the battle for the River Po in 1945 nearly a million German soldiers surrendered. The first mass capitulation of World War II.

It was the triumphant culmination of a long and bloody Italian campaign that had seen none of the much publicised and dramatic advances of other fronts. Italy was an inch-by-inch, mud and blood struggle marked by strategic mistakes and confusions at the top.

But at the Po it all came right. The Allies perfected their co-operation and achieved against the odds a stunning surprise and victory.

All this, Brian Harpur describes. But much more: as a junior officer he was there. He tells it as it was, in terms which anybody who was not there will easily understand. His is a memorable account of the grim realities of battle for the ordinary soldier: the mud, the mines and the shelling. The sheer, end-of-tether fatigue, and the comradeship.

'It would be difficult to better Brian Harpur's evocation of the combined doggedness and weary resignation that carried the Allies forward'

The Times

HODDER AND STOUGHTON PAPERBACKS

T. BOONE PICKENS JR

BOONE

He's made a fortune, he's big news but he's still an outsider.

In the boardrooms of American big business, he's feared and abused. But to many small investors and shareholders, he's a folk hero. He's challenged a series of huge companies – Gulf Oil, Phillips, Unocal – in deals that have changed the structure of big business in the United States.

Scathingly critical of much of the corporate establishment, he is contemptuous of the lazy, fat cat executives with their private jets and country club lifestyles, all paid for by shareholders they ignore.

He started out on his own in 1954. He was 26 and his first deal was worth $2,500. In 30 years he has created and built up Mesa Petroleum into a $3 billion company. This is how he did it.

Tough, witty, exciting and very personal, *Boone* is an eye-opening, provocative examination of the world of investment bankers, *arbitrageurs*, corporate raiders and takeovers.'

'His memoirs are just the best effort yet in a flourishing autobiographical sub-genre'

Financial Times

HODDER AND STOUGHTON PAPERBACKS

JUDGE JAMES PICKLES

STRAIGHT FROM THE BENCH

Judge James Pickles is a very unusual judge.

He says what he thinks and he won't shut up, even when it gets him into trouble. He thinks that there is a lot wrong with our legal system and that things won't get better unless someone makes a fuss. For instance:

* Do politics play a part when judges are appointed?
* How independent are judges anyway?
* Are the long – and often harrowing – delays in Crown Court cases really necessary?
* Plea-bargaining: shouldn't its existence be admitted and some proper rules be worked out?
* Juries: is it time to make some changes?

Judge Pickles never minces his words. He believes that much of our judicial system has to be modernised and modernised fast. Traditionalist attitudes on the part of all too many judges have to be altered. If not, then public confidence in our judicial system may be lost.

'It is refreshing to have a judge who seeks to justify the ways of judges to men. If Judge Pickles didn't exist John Mortimer would have to invent him'
New Society

'He has made an *important* contribution to an important debate and deserves our praise for doing so.'
Ludovic Kennedy, The Independent

HODDER AND STOUGHTON PAPERBACKS

DUFF HART-DAVIS

HITLER'S OLYMPICS

For Hitler, the Berlin Olympics of 1936 were a triumph of propaganda and deception.

Anti-Jewish notices and slogans were carefully, temporarily removed. The ceremonial and the mass crowd scenes were stage managed with military precision. Nationalistic fervour was whipped up as the real, evil nature of the regime was hidden. Barely a half-hour's journey from the stadium, Oranienburg concentration camp was already packed.

As sport and politics were ruthlessly forced together, as press reports and Berlin-based diplomats repeatedly warned of what was happening, in spite of protests – particularly from the Jewish community in the USA – the organisers of the Olympic movement blindly and blandly refused to see or acknowledge the truth.

The Nazis had their victory, yet a twenty-two year old black sprinter shattered not only records but the overweening mood of Aryan triumphalism.

The 1936 Olympics were Hitler's Games – and Jesse Owens' also.

'Duff Hart-Davis's book on that incredible year in sport is essential reading for all of us'
Financial Times

HODDER AND STOUGHTON PAPERBACKS

MORE TITLES AVAILABLE FROM
HODDER AND STOUGHTON PAPERBACKS

ARMAND HAMMER
with NEIL LYNDON

☐ 42446 X Hammer: Witness To History £4.99

ANTHONY SUMMERS AND
STEPHEN DORRIL

☐ 42973 9 Honeytrap £3.50

DICK WILSON

☐ 42215 7 The Sun At Noon £3.95

BRIAN HARPUR

☐ 42968 2 The Impossible Victory £2.95

T. BOONE PICKENS JR

☐ 42978 4 Boone £3.95

JUDGE JAMES PICKLES

☐ 42271 8 Straight From The Bench £2.95

DUFF HART-DAVIS

☐ 42648 9 Hitler's Olympics: The
1936 Games £2.95

*All these books are available at your local bookshop or
newsagent, or can be ordered direct from the publisher. Just
tick the titles you want and fill in the form below.*

Prices and availability subject to change without notice.

Hodder and Stoughton Paperbacks, P.O. Box 11, Falmouth,
Cornwall.

Please send cheque or postal order, and allow the following for
postage and packing:

U.K. – 55p for one book, plus 22p for the second book, and 14p for
each additional book ordered up to a £1.75 maximum.

B.F.P.O. and EIRE – 55p for the first book, plus 22p for the second
book, and 14p per copy for the next 7 books, 8p per book thereafter.

OTHER OVERSEAS CUSTOMERS – £1.00 for the first book, plus 25p
per copy for each additional book.

Name ....

Address ....

....